BRENNEN GREGORY

# HIDING ON THE PLAINS

## *CHANGE LED, SELF-DISCOVERY CAME NEXT, & SELF-BELIEF FOLLOWED*

*First published by The Awakened Creator 2025*



*First edition*

*ISBN: 979-8-218-83006-9*

*This book was professionally typeset on Reedsy.*
*Find out more at reedsy.com*

# Contents


DISCLAIMER 1
FRONT COVER EXPLAINED 2
PREFACE 3
INTRODUCTION 6
SECTION I: MY DRINKING SAGA 9
- MY DRINKING HISTORY 9
- MY DRINKING IDENTITY 11
- MY LONG-OVERDUE APOLOGY 12
- MOMENT #1: RESIGNATION LETTER 15
- THREE PILLARS THAT SPEARHEADED A LIFE OF SOBRIETY 16

SECTION II-A: TWO YEARS SOBER 19
- FIRST SOBERCATION: JULY 8, 2023 19
- SLEEPING BEAR DUNES NATIONAL LAKESHORE OVERLOOKING BEAUTIFUL LAKE MICHIGAN 21
- THE SIEGE: AUGUST 13, 2023 22
- POST-SIEGE 23
- MONKEY BARS > BREN 24
- VISITING HOME AFTER TWO YEARS: AUGUST 30, 2023 24
- MOMENT #2: KELLY'S ADVICE 26
- ONE YEAR SOBER: DECEMBER 8, 2023 28
- 'TWAS THE NIGHT BEFORE CHRISTMAS 2023: DECEMBER 24, 2023 29
- GRANDMA SHARON: MARCH 20, 2024 30
- THE STRONGEST WAVE: JULY 13, 2024 32
- MOVING: AUGUST 6, 2024 33
- MOVING (ONE WEEK IN): AUGUST 13, 2024 33

COMING HOME: SEPTEMBER 15, 2024 34
TAKING THE ROAD LESS TRAVELED: OCTOBER 22, 2024 35
WHY AM I NEVER THE SAME PERSON EVERY DAY? NOVEMBER 06, 2024 36
TWO YEARS SOBER: DECEMBER 09, 2024 37
SECTION II-B: ALCOHOL REINTRODUCTION—FIRST SIX MONTHS 40
OKLAHOMA TRIP DECEMBER 17, 2024 40
ANITA THORPE'S RESPONSE 44
GOING FOR A TEST RUN IN NEW MEXICO: MARCH 20, 2025 45
MOMENT #3: LITTLE RAVEN 47
SIMPLE GESTURES MATTER: MARCH 29, 2025 48
MOMENT #4: DON'T DISCOUNT THE IMPORTANCE OF A FIRST IMPRESSION 49
TYLER JAMES BIG BOW 51
DWELLING IN QUANDARY: APRIL 9, 2025 52
MY LETTER TO SOUTHWEST KS: APRIL 15, 2025 53
STILL A WORK IN PROGRESS: MAY 7, 2025 54
6 MONTHS IN: JUNE 9, 2025 56
A LETTER TO MY YOUNGER SELF: JUNE 28, 2025 57
MY BIRTHDAY MEANS VERY LITTLE WITHOUT OTHERS: JULY 2, 2025 60
PINCH ME, I MUST BE DREAMING: JULY 22, 2025 61
SECTION III: THE MEAT & POTATOES 63
SUGAR 63
GAMBLING (WRITTEN IN APRIL 2023) 63
GAMBLING (6 MONTHS LATER) 65
LOVING KINDNESS 65
READING 66
MUSIC 68
WORK 69

A FORMER PATIENT'S LITTLE SISTER DREW THIS ILLUSTRATION OF ME 71
MOMENT #5: MY WORDS ONE WEEK BEFORE ENTERING SOBRIETY 72
VOICE MEMOS 72
SPEAKING TO THE FELLAS 74
INSPIRATION MAGNIFIED 75
KEEP A FEW RECEIPTS 77
YOU'RE MORE RESILIENT THAN YOU THINK 78
RELICS OF RESILIENCE 79
FIVE TRAVEL ESSENTIALS ON MY SELF-DISCOVERY JOURNEY 79
THE GRAND CRESCENDO 88
ACKNOWLEDGEMENTS, AKA THE WONDERS OF MY WORLD 95
WORKS CITED 98
*About the Author* 99

# DISCLAIMER

This book is a memoir, shared for storytelling and personal reflection. It is not intended to provide medical, psychological, psychiatric, or legal advice. The author is not a licensed professional, and nothing in this book should be taken as a substitute for professional care, diagnosis, treatment, or legal counsel. Readers are encouraged to seek qualified help for their individual needs.

This memoir includes discussions of alcohol use disorder, recovery, and mental health struggles. Experiences vary widely, and what is described here may not be safe or appropriate for everyone.

If you or someone you know needs immediate support, the following free, confidential resources are available:

- **Suicide & Crisis Lifeline (U.S.):** Call or text **988**
- https://988lifeline.org
- **SAMHSA National Helpline (Substance Use & Mental Health, U.S.):**
- **1-800-662-HELP (4357)**
- https://www.samhsa.gov/find-help/national-helpline
- **International crisis resources:**
- https://www.opencounseling.com/suicide-hotlines

If you are in immediate danger, please contact your local emergency number right away.

# FRONT COVER EXPLAINED

The hand-drawn image you see on the cover of this book is no other than yours truly, seated in "the thinker" pose, a gift I received during my clinical rotation in occupational therapy assistant (OTA) school. COTA is my current job title and stands for Certified Occupational Therapist Assistant. Back in 2018, I was in my last semester of school and finishing up my second-to-last clinical rotation when I acquired this thoughtful piece of art. On my last day, my supervisor presented me with a religious book, a cantaloupe, and a card. The front of the card featured the hand-drawn image you see on the front of this book; the inside of the card read "a book meant for the thinking person, and a cantaloupe! Good luck, kid."

Not that long ago, I ran across an image of *The Thinker* statue, and my attention immediately reverted to that card. I realized this pose represented a deep thinker and philosophically minded person. In the span of three months, my supervisor saw characteristics in me I didn't see in myself. I appreciate her insight, and her gift serves as a daily reminder to remember who you are. I am Brennen "the thinker." Thinking paralyzed many aspects of me for years, but it also helped me reach heights I never thought I could.

# PREFACE

Giving has always been near and dear to my heart. From an early age, I showed an inclination to help others. Through small acts and gestures, I have gone through life eager to help people in any way I can. Here, I give my story, my vulnerabilities, my experiences, my highs & lows, my wisdom, and my heart in this book.

Giving it my all for this book was a given, but finding my "why" proved more elusive.

At first, I was hung up on proving to others that I could produce something meaningful. I wanted notoriety and everything that came with it. My thoughts were focused on climbing the ladder of success. I still have lofty expectations for myself, and not to pooh-pooh that way of thinking, but I needed another driver in the driver's seat. The driver in this book is impact. Impact that gives someone a sense of comfort, belonging, or the inspiration to grow. Impact that leads to change, sympathy for the person next to you, or a connection with someone who inspires you. I needed to find my modus operandi early on, so I could write with the foundation already in place.

I needed to find two more occupants to tag along for this journey. This writing process became a therapeutic outlet for me, as I treated every writing session as an opportunity to learn more about myself. This book also gave me a platform to express myself like never before. I wanted to track my mishaps, my growth, and my evolution as a human being and author. I'm not ashamed to say I wrote this book for me, too. The therapeutic outlet and surveillance tracker were the two lucky occupants who secured the last seats in the vehicle. The vehicle was ready to go, but I had trouble disengaging the emergency brake.

A lot of self-doubt seeped in during this writing process. Self-questioning and second-guessing surfaced repeatedly. What qualified me to be a spokesman for change? What's so special about my story that gives it any merit? These types of thoughts hung around for what seemed like forever. I finally had my breakthrough when my desire to share my story superseded my feelings of self-doubt. It was all part of the process. My thoughts took a sharp U-turn as I started to ask myself, "Why not me?" I don't think I am better than anyone, less than anyone, or even equal to anyone.

I am one of one, and so are you. I am uniquely qualified to share my story and speak on changes in my life. I speak on change from very different backgrounds and perspectives. I speak on change as a man who is black, white, and has some Hispanic heritage. I speak on change as a man who isn't the manliest of men and is vulnerable enough to acknowledge that. I speak on change as a man with "soft" features—a touch of sensitivity and plenty of compassion to go around. I speak on change as a man who lives alone, unwed, and childless. I speak on change as a man who has felt lost in this world and lacked an identity. I speak on change as a man who struggled in school and had some learning challenges along the way.

I speak on change as a man who arm wrestles with the narrative that he is capable of extraordinary feats. I speak on change as a man who has overcome many obstacles in life, none bigger than surviving a collapsed lung at birth. Lastly, I speak on change as someone who made a significant transformation in life and is still discovering who they are.

Giving up alcohol was a catalyst for growth and self-discovery. It revitalized my spirit and gave me a new outlook on life. Somewhere along the road, I lost who I was, and giving up alcohol forced me to change course. I spent so many years looking to please others that I neglected the man in the mirror. I needed to discover myself, find what makes me tick, and learn to love myself. I only felt happy when I was doing things for others, even though most of my time was spent alone. For many years, I carried a deeply ingrained sense of self-disregard.

This book is presented in three sections. Section I, **MY DRINKING SAGA**, details my drinking history, my drinking identity, and the three pillars that initiated a life of sobriety. Section II is broken up into two subsections, A & B. Section II-A, **TWO YEARS SOBER**, chronicles my two years of sobriety, with monumental life events depicted and documented in real time. Section II-B, **ALCOHOL REINTRODUCTION: FIRST SIX MONTHS**, reveals the honeymoon phase with alcohol and a growing self-belief. Section III, **THE MEAT & POTATOES**, covers my helpful activities, my guilty pleasures, and my take-it-or-leave-it advice. I also sprinkle in some powerful "moments" that stood out while writing this book. I have these sections to keep the book somewhat organized, but, to be honest, it's a tangled mess of experiences, thoughts, feelings, and emotions. This book is very symbolic of what occurs in my mind from moment to moment.

I never followed a writing schedule and only wrote when I had a scratch to itch. For the most part, this book is in total disarray, and I wouldn't have it any other way. Early on, I tried to stretch my words with long, drawn-out stories, but it wasn't me. My writing style is short and straight to the point.

My confidence will come and go throughout the book as I move through different developmental stages of self. There's a high chance I will repeat myself once or twice, which I guess isn't a bad thing if you are trying to write things into existence. This book won't be elegant, but it will contain real substance. New concepts are constantly being introduced in this book, as I find my place in this world. This book serves as my "loud" moment in life. The days of me hiding on the plains are over. For the first time in my life, I'm pushing my voice and my story to the front of the line, so stay awhile!

# INTRODUCTION

On December 7, 2022, I woke up disheveled, in a daze, and full of regret. Per usual, I had blacked out after a long night of drinking. I say long night, but really it was three to four hours of drinking with bad intentions. Drinking myself into oblivion was not how I saw the night going, but when things go awry, the bottle is still present and accounted for.

Earlier that day, I received word that no man wants to hear when he is attempting to court a young lady. This young lady informed me that she would not make it to the planned dinner we had scheduled, and she was no longer interested. Hearing this news was a crushing blow to my psyche. I met this young lady on a dating app, and let's hope I never have to set foot in those treacherous waters again. My ego took over right away, and I grew spiteful. Throughout the day, all I could think about was getting out of work and getting to the closest drinking establishment.

Once I got out of work, I could faintly hear Buffalo Wild Wings (BDubs) calling my name. On this day, they had discounted wings, but the main draw was the $4 Bud Lights. After work, I made my way over to BDubs. I had a few beers with my wings, but once the wings were gone, I could finally get down to business. My sole attention then turned to guzzling beer after beer. The feelings of disappointment from earlier in the day began to slowly vanish, as did my memory. I know I drove home and went to bed at some point, but everything in between is a blur. Home for me at the time was a single bedroom in the basement of a co-worker's house. I had worked with this co-worker for a couple of years, and even briefly worked with her husband.

When I came home late, I turned the calm, relaxing environment into a hostile scene. I became a repulsive little prick to the people who were sharing their home with me, rent-free. At some point, I made my way to my room, hopped in bed, and passed out. When I woke up the next morning, after gaining my bearings, I reached over for my phone. On my phone, I saw a text message from my co-worker's husband. Before reading the message, I already knew what it would entail. You see, this wasn't my first rodeo, and hearing about my escapades from the night before was becoming all too common. I was living in his house, so I had no choice but to face the music. His text message stated that my behavior the previous night would not be tolerated and that my living arrangement with them was on thin ice. I apologized and acknowledged that I had worn out my welcome. I had come home frequently in a buzzed or drunken state, but my gradual arrogance and lack of respect were understandably no longer tolerable.

Earlier, when I lived with my co-worker, we had additional roommates. One of the roommates was a woman happily in a long-distance relationship. Occasionally, all the roommates would drink, listen to music, and celebrate the weekend, as most people in their mid-twenties do. One night, I stayed up drinking late into the night, long after everybody went to bed. I decided to text my female roommate to see if she was awake. I waited, but never got a reply, and what I did next brings me shame to this day. I made an unwanted advance, and rightfully so, was met with resistance. This severe lapse in judgment led me to violate a sacred boundary. All the commotion woke the other roommates, who eventually heard what happened. In a matter of minutes, I had managed to make every single person in that house uncomfortable and wary of me.

Not to gloss over this incident, but let's get back to the morning of December 7, 2022. After you add up all these transgressions, it makes sense that my living arrangement was in serious jeopardy. That initial wave of embarrassment washed over me as I got ready for work. As I got to work, I quickly realized I didn't have the dignity to face my co-worker, so I faked being sick to get out. Before I left town, I started calling around for any available rental options ASAP. There was going to be a discussion that night, and I had to face the reality that I might get kicked out. I came back to the house and sat in stillness.

Pent-up emotions were being released, and I sobbed uncontrollably for a couple of hours. I really contemplated my life and what direction it was heading in. During this emotional awakening, it became apparent that I needed help. I wanted to gain control of my life, and later that day, I called a co-worker who was an Alcoholics Anonymous (AA) member. I let her know I needed help, and I had a desire to stop drinking alcohol. That evening, we met up and attended an AA meeting. What a surreal moment—I was taken aback by the stories I was hearing. In a room full of strangers, I shared my struggles with alcohol coherently and articulately. Some higher power came over me, and I had absolute clarity in that moment. I finally reached the mental space where I saw living a sober life as a real possibility.

# SECTION I: MY DRINKING SAGA

## MY DRINKING HISTORY

My first encounter with alcohol came during childhood—and I can explain. I must have been three or four years old, and I remember it clear as day, sitting on my dad's lap, surrounded by my mom's side of the family, at my aunt and uncle's house. My dad was attempting to drink a beer, but my curious mind and little fingers kept interrupting his plans. Dad finally gave in and let me see what all the fuss was about. He let me sip his beer, and after that sip, I let him drink in peace. As most might expect, my preschool taste buds were not too fond of alcohol. To some degree, my early life experience softened my exuberance when it came to alcohol.

Alcohol and I didn't meet again until my junior year in high school. One night, I was kickin' it with my cousin and good friend when that hard stuff made another appearance. We started playing beer pong, and I assumed the clear liquid in those red Solo cups was water. If you knew me at that age, you wouldn't be surprised by my assumption based on my level of innocence. I immediately realized I wasn't drinking water when that intense burning liquid, which we call vodka, entered my throat. When my number was called the rest of the night, I gutted it out and took a few more swigs of vodka. A few swigs would pale in comparison to what awaited me in college.

Going off to college in Kearney, Nebraska, felt like I was entering a new world, even though I was only five hours away from home. Most incoming first-year students look forward to the drinking scene, but it was so far off my radar when I stepped on campus. I had no pulse on alcohol; I didn't even know if I liked it. Every drinking experience in high school stemmed from looking to blend it. I didn't drink from a place of natural curiosity, that would come later. The University of Nebraska at Kearney's abbreviation was UNK, and those three letters meant nothing to me until I learned of the school's moniker. You can't spell drunk without UNK, and I quickly adopted the school moniker. By day two on campus, I was already finding house parties with my roommate and eventual best friend, Aric.

As you might imagine, the main draw at these parties was alcohol, with the pretty girls being a close second. Pop culture tells us that drinking is a normal college experience, and I don't think I really comprehended that notion until I stepped foot into that first house party. Looking to fit in and really embrace "college life" meant I was looking to drink.

Those first few weeks of school were a blur; eager to spread my wings meant I didn't fully grasp the power of alcohol. I can still remember the aftertaste of brandy that lingered on my freshman year toothbrush. The frequency and intensity of drinking gradually increased as the year went on. I wish I could show you the quality of notes I took in my 8 a.m. Mon-Wed-Fri class. I was often sleeping off a bad hangover, but when I wasn't asleep, my notes looked like a cave man wrote them. By Thanksgiving of my first year, I had already quit the track team (bad idea), and partying was what I looked forward to most. I was in full-on party mode, and when every weekend rolled around, I was getting obliterated. Shoot, forget just the weekend; I was getting drunk during the week, too. I continued this trend for roughly two years before I realized I needed to go back home.

I was self-aware enough to realize I wasn't focused on school, and I was getting more and more enthralled with alcohol. I moved back to Colorado, but the two years I was away, I established a drinking routine that centered around parties on the weekend and escaping through alcohol. That thing that scared me early on was my inability to drink moderately. In those early days, I drank alcohol to get drunk. During my twenties, alcohol became a core element of my identity.

# MY DRINKING IDENTITY

As time wore on, I proudly took on the role of a "drinker." It was during these years that I exemplified a warped sense of self. I had convinced myself that I was a big drinker, and I had an image to uphold.

At parties or outings, I was the guy keeping my empty beers on the table to show off my drinking abilities. I was constantly calling out what number beer I was on or comparing with my drinking compadres. Aric can tell you how infatuated I became with who was drinking more, who got drunk first, and so forth. I wanted to show I could excel at something, and during many of those years, it was drinking. I never grew physically dependent on alcohol, but it was constantly on my mind. Take going out to eat, for example. I usually had a few beers. When the weekend rolled around, I still carried the college mindset to get drunk and let loose. When I had a date, when I was celebrating, when I went on vacation, and so on, I was drinking.

In those early years, I would say I was mainly a celebratory drinker (social outings, events, parties, etc.), but then I started to gradually drink more as an emotional escape. I began to drink to numb my feelings, insecurities, and negative thoughts, all while seeking that temporary relief. Any time I had alcohol in my system, I felt like I was someone else. I had a hard time accepting the sober me, and I liked that early drinking version of me.

Alcohol raised all aspects of me until I came up to that line. Once that line was crossed, all bets were off. At that point, I was at the mercy of alcohol, and from an outsider's perspective, it must have been a spectacle to see. I don't want to embellish my stories and make it seem like bad things happened every time I drank, but it was still an unsettling pattern. Some nights I would keep things to a low roar, and other nights I would unleash pandemonium. Hard alcohol led the way for many of those heavily intoxicated nights. At times, I could get too mouthy, out of control, pushy, aggressive, belligerent, and reckless. Most of my regrettable moments in life have come from this dark side. Unfortunately, many of these bad nights ended with me being the topic of discussion the next day.

These routines became so embedded that I became numb to the consequences. God must have been on my side all these years, because these consequences never took the criminal law route. I don't know how I eluded a DUI charge all those years, but I probably should have woke up in the slammer a time or two. I had taken short hiatuses from alcohol before, but after some time, my old drinking habits would come slithering back. I continued to take the quick-fix approach towards drinking and had no luck. To give myself a chance to grow meant I needed to make a vow. I had plenty of issues to address, but one stood at the top of the list. Refraining from alcohol for a considerable amount of time seemed like my only feasible option. I had to get uncomfortable to grow, and that can be a scary proposition. I knew this would be a tough ask, but somewhere deep inside, I knew I had to make this decision. I had no inkling of what waited for me on the other side, but I was game. My identity was so tied up in alcohol; could I really give it up?

## MY LONG-OVERDUE APOLOGY

Before we move on, I need to atone for my actions. I did some despicable things that nobody would be proud of. I can't change what happened, but I can start rectifying my faults with sincerity. I've apologized in the past, but not from a clear-minded and reflective state. I've had ample time to think about my actions, and, as the title says, it's been long overdue. Apologies, where do I start?

First and foremost, I want to apologize to two of my ex-girlfriends. These two come to mind because they both felt the brunt of my aggression when under the influence of alcohol. They were the two who, behind the scenes, dealt with the worst side of me. I'm referring to the side of me that, at times, became physically abusive. Putting my hands on anyone is totally unacceptable, and I must live with that. I wish you two the very best, and from the bottom of my heart, I am sorry.

My family has been there from the start and stuck by me when I was at my worst. Nobody close to me has abandoned or shunned me because of my drinking, and I am grateful for that. I am so sorry for all the embarrassment and shame I have brought to our family. Thank you for loving me through thick and thin, and I'm sorry you're learning about some of my horrible moments in a book. I'm still that little Bren that wants to make you all proud. I love you all.

I have lost countless friends due to my drinking. Some friends had seen enough and moved on with their lives, while others never received a reply from me out of embarrassment. Back in the day, it was easier for me to lose a friend than to acknowledge my Achilles' heel. I cherished those close friendships, and I often catch myself wondering how they're doing in life. I was too stubborn to apologize and too prideful to admit my wrongs. I am glad those days are behind me, because with 100% sincerity, I can say, I am sorry. I am sorry for my behavior, my actions, and my hurtful words. I am sorry for abandoning those friendships as if they meant nothing. I plan to send some copies of this book to friends I've lost contact with, as a window into my past. I understand more work must be done to reconcile friendships, but that will give me a good starting point. When that time comes, I look forward to reconnecting. Before we move on, I want to apologize to the friend who never left, Aric. Since we're on the topic of friends, I want to apologize to you for having to put up with my drinking shenanigans.

The next group of people that come to mind are the innocent bystanders. The folks I had no connection with, but who unfortunately crossed my path. One night, a childhood friend and I grabbed a post-drinking meal at IHOP in Lincoln, Nebraska. Something didn't settle in my stomach, and I quickly bolted for the bathroom. As I entered the bathroom, I saw a man standing with his back towards me, peeing in the urinal, minding his own business. To this day, I can't fathom what compelled me to do what I did next. The contents in my stomach were quickly on the way up, and I needed to find a toilet ASAP. Instead of going towards the sink as I should have, I went straight to the urinal where the man was. The poor man never saw me coming, and I hurled all over his back. I mean, it was a sizable amount of vomit covering his entire back. I deserved a beating like no other that night, but the man handled this situation a lot better than most would. I consider myself a pretty laid-back, friendly person, but I feel I would have reacted in some way. I never got the opportunity to apologize, and if you're out there somewhere, I'm sorry, man.

The other innocent bystander is an older woman in Jacksonville, Florida. A sports internship (a degree I never used) brought me to Jacksonville in the fall of 2013. A night started with drinking and ended with us overlooking Jacksonville Beach from a hotel. On the way to the hotel, we stopped and picked up some cocaine. In my intoxicated state, I snorted some. Things in the hotel got strange, and I left quickly. I won't detail what happened, but I was losing my faculties and vaguely remember stumbling and getting a ride home from a cop.

When I woke up the next morning, the shoes I was wearing the night before and my phone were nowhere to be found. I called my phone, only to have an elderly woman answer and tell me she had seen my phone and shoes on her porch. She figured my phone and shoes had been stolen and somehow ended up on her porch. I knew right away that wasn't the case, but I was too ashamed to tell her the truth. I have no recollection of this, but I'm positive I was trying to enter her house (which I've done before and resulted in having the cops called on me).

I believe I mistook her house for mine on my stumble home, thinking the porch would be my bed. I passed out, then realized I wasn't home and returned to the street, where a cop saw me. I don't remember what I said, but I got home safely, though I could have been jailed for trespassing. The next day, I retrieved my phone and shoes from her house, which is three doors down. I never apologized for troubling her. What pains me most is how worried she was about my lost belongings. I'm sorry for causing worry and for stepping on her property at night.

Lastly, I want to apologize to anyone whom I affected negatively, whether it was drinking-related or not. I hope you sense my sincerity, and I wish everyone the very best. Before I could board the sober train, I had to reach acceptance, take accountability, and share my struggles with alcohol.

# MOMENT #1: RESIGNATION LETTER

## Resignation Letter

From: Brennen Gregory

brengreg1990@yahoo.com

To: Wesley Medical Center

550 N Hillside St

Wichita, KS 67214

To Whom It May Concern,

I (Brennen Gregory) working as a Certified Occupational Therapy Assistant would like to inform you that I will be resigning from my position immediately due to personal reasons. These reasons result in me relocating immediately for the time being to get the necessary support and help I need during this tough time.

I truly appreciate you giving me the opportunity to work at Wesley. Although my time here was brief, I was able to gain a lot of valuable experience and insight. I will be contacting HR during this process as well. I will leave my badge and parking pass in my locker. I apologize for the abrupt timing of this announcement, thank you for the opportunity.

Sincerely,

Brennen Gregory

In the summer of 2022, I took a crack at living in Wichita, Kansas. I could never get my bearings, and the setup I had was not conducive to my mental health. My drinking and erratic behavior started to escalate as I tried to numb my existence. Having no one to turn to further isolated me, and I fell into a depression.

I quickly relocated back to Southwest KS, but the alcohol issues still followed. Even though I filled one void (being back with my work family), I was still missing my own living arrangement, and I didn't like the marital status I carried at that time (single). I was glad to be back in Southwest KS, but that didn't necessarily solve all my problems. I resigned from my job, but I was gradually becoming more resigned to life. I bring up this story to show you where my life was before the decision to give up alcohol and to remind you that moving doesn't necessarily cure all your problems. Each time I move, I am reminded of that fact.

## THREE PILLARS THAT SPEARHEADED A LIFE OF SOBRIETY

### ACCEPTANCE

Arriving at the stage where I accepted my drinking struggles was a game-changer. At some point in my childhood, I developed a perfection complex regarding my self-image. Because I lacked confidence, I had to cover up my insecurities by maintaining an angelic image. Even though I happen to be a very nice person by nature, I didn't need anything to derail my boy next door persona. Having drinking issues didn't align with who I was, or so I thought. As I write this, I can't help but self-analyze: I was so consumed with how I was portrayed that I couldn't separate who I was from who I wasn't. I didn't want to accept that I had character flaws. This problematic drinker seemed like a figment of my imagination. It couldn't be me, could it? My thoughts wavered for years, but I never reached total acceptance until December 7, 2022. That day, I finally accepted that alcohol was not for me.

## ACCOUNTABILITY

It just so happened that the day I decided to quit drinking alcohol was also the day I took full accountability for my life. Up until that point, I always had a rebuttal, or a "yeah, but" excuse for my drinking-related behavior. I would always conjure up justifications, either externally for those who witnessed my drinking etiquette (sarcasm) or internally for myself. I would hear or be reminded of my conduct from those close to me, and feel that initial wave of embarrassment, which would slowly trickle away over time. I was in this habit loop of bad drunken nights followed by chill bouts of drinking independently. Then, when I filled that courage tank up, I would get drunk and yet again make a fool of myself. I remember my mom and sister talking to me about my drinking and the concerns they had, but I always felt I had things under control. I was a very obedient child growing up, and I would always consider the feelings of others, but I also had this arrogance when it came to drinking. A tiny sliver of me didn't care what others thought in those drunken states, and I always felt I had the nice-guy-most-of-the-time card in my back pocket.

Growing up, I always thought it was others' responsibility to push me into areas that piqued my interest. I was not self-motivated or curious enough to poke and prod on my own. This trend of waiting for others to guide me in the right direction continued in life when I had my drinking problem. I was going to push the boundaries with drinking while secretly waiting for someone to set me straight. I say that now, but if I'm being honest with myself, I don't know if I was at a point in my life when I would consider giving up drinking. I've learned over time and through this process that it's not anyone's responsibility where I go or what I do with my life. Ultimately, that's up to me, and I've got to find the desire to make my own change. I haven't always been able to say this, but I don't blame anyone for the way my life has turned out. The past is the past. I'm standing here now, where my two feet are, and taking accountability for my life.

Making a change in your own self-interest will allow you to be the best for yourself and others. Nobody is responsible for you; you are accountable for your life, remember that.

## SHARING

The night I attended an AA meeting, the usual social anxiety that torments me simply went out the window. This setting was the first time I voiced my true feelings about my struggles with alcohol. In that moment, I felt a more profound sense of self and was open to vulnerability. Attending that AA meeting was a stepping-stone moment for me and served as my first semi-public platform.

I am incredibly grateful for the opportunity to attend an AA meeting and for the resources they made available. Anyone who wants to stop drinking should strongly consider AA, as it will support their recovery efforts. I'll never forget the night I attended an AA meeting and shared my alcohol story. Not to brush aside this momentous occasion, but these kinds of dialogues would become a recurring theme for me in the future. I kept my struggles with alcohol so tight to the vest for years that I was filled with excitement at the thought of sharing with people. I was ready to let people know about my struggles with alcohol, and it helped from a therapeutic standpoint to talk about it. For years, I had tried to dismiss these talks from happening, and now I was making up for lost time. It also helped to keep me accountable and a man of my word if I told others I was committing to a life of sobriety. I have no problem delving into my past with alcohol, and with total transparency, I can finally call myself out without shame. I finally had some internal revelations encompassing alcohol, but now came life after alcohol. I was motivated for change, but how would things go once that initial excitement fades?

# SECTION II-A: TWO YEARS SOBER

## FIRST SOBERCATION: JULY 8, 2023

For my 33rd birthday, I took a trip with my mom and her fiancè to Traverse City, Michigan.

I knew the airport was going to be a challenge because of the association I had made with airports and alcohol. Because of this, I intentionally chose an earlier departure time. I am less reluctant to drink earlier in the day, and who knows, the airport restaurants and bars could be closed. Another thing I planned to do was arrive at the airport an hour and fifteen minutes before my departure time. I knew that decision could backfire, but I wanted to set myself up for success, and in my experiences, I've always made it to the gate with plenty of time to spare.

In the weeks leading up to my trip, I had pondered the idea of using marijuana as a substitute for alcohol. I can count on two hands how many times I've smoked marijuana in my life, and almost all those times were in college. On top of that, whenever I smoked marijuana, I was usually already drunk long before I took that first hit. It was hard to say how it really made me feel. In my head, I went back and forth on whether to get some edibles before my trip, and ultimately decided to stop at the dispensary. I had no experience in buying marijuana, let alone knowing the different types. So, as you can imagine, I was utterly clueless walking into that dispensary.

I let the bud tender know I was looking to relax on my flight to Michigan, and I let them lead the way. I followed their recommendation and picked out some edibles I thought would do the trick. So, I took two edibles, and after thirty minutes, I turned into an overthinking, paranoid, and restless individual who never felt relaxed at any point or time.

The effects of the marijuana wore off by the time I landed in Grand Rapids, Michigan. I went out to Michigan the day before Mom and her fiancé, and I was unsure how this day would go. As soon as I landed, I took an Uber to my hotel. After unpacking my belongings and washing off the psychological remnants of the marijuana, I headed out for dinner. Remarkably, my appetite for alcohol was not too pervasive. It was only one day, but for that day, I was able to stave off alcohol. The day I was most worried about turned out to go just the way I wanted.

Mom and her fiancé arrived the next day, and then the fun really began! On the drive to Traverse City, I told Mom and her fiancé to treat this vacation like any other. If they felt inclined to have some alcohol, then go ahead and enjoy some alcohol. I didn't want my sobriety to affect any decisions they made regarding alcohol. My mom, being who she is, said something along the lines of, "Great, now we have the permission to go crazy." She was obviously joking, but it was a relief for me to tell them to enjoy themselves. I didn't want my decision to affect them, and I needed to test my commitment to sobriety. It's easy to remain sober when you're not in the thick of it, but I can't let sobriety impact me from living my life and exploring. The time was going to come sooner rather than later, and I handled my first sobercation way better than I expected. There was one night when mom and her fiancé had some wine, but because my mood was naturally lifted, I felt zero pressure to drink alcohol. Alcohol really became a distant thought on this trip because I welcomed all the experiences and the people I shared those experiences with.

From this trip, I learned you don't need any substance (drugs or alcohol) to enjoy a vacation. What I needed was someone I'm close with to bring me up while I'm still on my journey to find myself. Mom made this trip fun just by being there and bringing her energy. Mom has always radiated an infectious energy that makes time with her lively and effortless. Having her fiancé around for comic relief didn't hurt either (sorry, guy). Being the butt of the joke is how our family initiates you. I've been a joke for years, so I know the feeling. All jokes aside, it was nice getting to know her fiancé—my eventual stepdad—on a deeper level. I'll never forget our day trip to Mackinac Island (mom was sick, as usual).

## SLEEPING BEAR DUNES NATIONAL LAKESHORE OVERLOOKING BEAUTIFUL LAKE MICHIGAN

## THE SIEGE: AUGUST 13, 2023

In about two hours, I will be running in my first obstacle course race, or whatever you call them. All I know is that I will be running a 5K race with twenty obstacles. These military-based obstacles are meant to test your physical abilities and mental strength. This race could not have come at a better time, given my recent increase in satisfaction from bodily movement. Challenging my body on the track, in the weight room, or doing a high-intensity workout with a weighted vest has brought me a euphoric high like no other. Having those internal dialogues of wanting to quit before the conclusion of a workout and overriding those thoughts that tell you to quit is the ultimate "feel good." Fighting through the pain and agony has never felt so rewarding.

I feel accomplished, and I am not afraid to say it. I am proud of myself. I couldn't care less how these workouts stack up to others. All I know is that busting my ass doing something uncomfortable and painful brings me a sense of strength and perseverance. It has been fun looking back and seeing how the variety and intensity of these workouts have changed since I've returned to a regular exercise regimen. I don't think I would have discovered this craving for pushing my physical limits had I not decided to quit drinking alcohol. Finding something that brings me internal joy and validation, along with a host of other benefits, is another reminder that I made the right decision. I never thought removing one unwanted habit could make me feel this way. I feel like I'm heading toward uncovering more passions and growth. If you find that thing that makes you feel good about yourself or proud, hold that thing tight and don't let it go. At this point, I know I crave hard physical movements, and I plan to keep it that way. Today marks another step up in physical challenge as I conquer "The Siege."

# POST-SIEGE

When I say I had no idea what to expect, I literally mean I had no idea what to expect. At one point in the race, I was about to flip a massive tractor tire when a volunteer showed me I only needed to jump in and out of it. Going from climbing a wooden ladder, swinging across a puddle of water, and finally crawling in the mud had my head spinning for the first half of the race. I distinctly remember veering back and forth a few times as I tried to regain my equilibrium. I didn't complete all the obstacles because I couldn't tap into my elementary school days. I could not conquer the deceptive monkey bars and was instead given the option to do the much easier ten push-ups. I have never felt more relieved to do ten push-ups in my life. As the race continued, I felt a greater sense of belonging and strength. I don't really know how to eloquently describe what I was feeling, but I felt in the zone and in my element. I finished with a strong kick because I noticed a guy gaining on me in the last little stretch. I wanted to run my race, but the competitive side of me took over, and I made sure I was not caught from behind. My first thought crossing the finish line let me know how far I'd come. My first thought wasn't relief that the race was over, but rather how I could improve my upper body strength to swing on the monkey bars.

## MONKEY BARS > BREN

## VISITING HOME AFTER TWO YEARS: AUGUST 30, 2023

I decided to go back home for my grandma's 78$^{th}$ birthday, and as that title states, I hadn't been home in over two years. This also happened to be my first trip back home as the sober me, which might have something to do with why I hadn't been home sooner. On my dad's side of the family, I always felt internal pressure to be highly successful—and, in my skewed mind, "perfect." Although my family didn't see most of my drinking issues, I feared my struggles would be exposed if I drank much around them.

That viewpoint led me to distance myself from my family, so I wouldn't feel pressured to visit. I can admit it now. My family has always been loving, supportive, and there for me, but I would be lying if I told you I always believed that. I tried to convince myself that I wasn't missed or loved, because those thoughts fit my motives at the time. I came home very seldom, to avoid the false embarrassment I felt and the low self-image I carried.

Each time I visited, I was not myself; I interacted very little and counted the hours until I could return home. I wanted to talk very little about myself, because (A) I felt I had very little to contribute, and (B) I did not want anything drinking-related brought up. The real me was someone who had drinking issues and was scared to disappoint and humiliate my family. Early on in my sobriety, I began having more in-depth thoughts about many situations and relationships in my life. Reconnecting and visiting my family back in Colorado became the utmost priority. It took me eight months into my sobriety to have the correct intentions on returning home. This version of me returning home was more confident in who he was, could share his drinking issues, and savor family time like the old days. Even though I had rehearsed how I would tell my family, I knew it would still be hard to do. The first test came before I arrived in Denver.

On the drive there, my dad texted me to ask if I would like to join him later for some drinks. It took me about five minutes to decide how to respond, but after that, I replied with the following text.

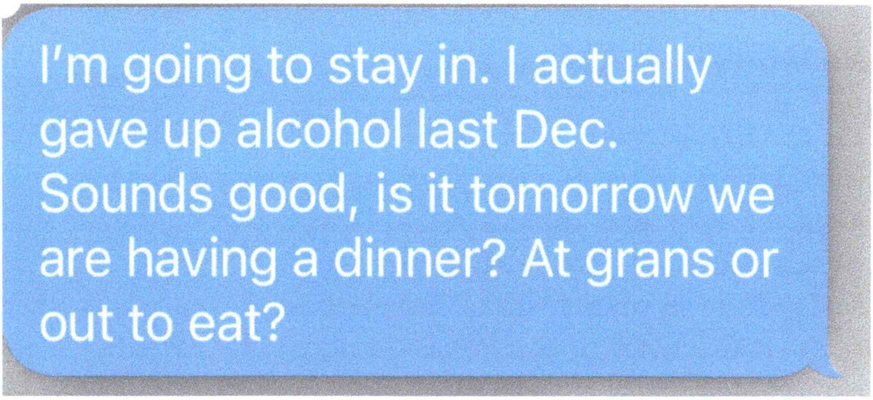

I'm going to stay in. I actually gave up alcohol last Dec. Sounds good, is it tomorrow we are having a dinner? At grans or out to eat?

As you can see, I was also trying to figure out what the dinner plans were for the next day. That was the first chunk of weight that was lifted off my shoulders. I had finally shared with someone on my dad's side of my family, which happened to be my dad, that I was sober from alcohol.

I didn't share my sobriety with every member, but I finally felt the remaining weight fall off the back of my shoulders. The topic of sobriety was discussed briefly with my dad and gran. The opportunity never arose to share with my brothers, cousins, or aunt, but I look forward to having those conversations if need be. As we all know, family news travels fast, and before long, everyone will know. Being around my family felt like the old days; I was completely comfortable and soaking it all up. I let my family know my intentions of moving back in the future and felt fully supported. I don't think I would have arrived at this place of self-growth, which in turn led to strengthening family relationships again, had I not decided to get sober. By no means do I have everything figured out, but I am taking steps in the right direction. Self-growth led me to gain more confidence in accepting myself, which in turn led me to share my vulnerabilities and feel close to my family again. This trickle-down effect stems from one life-changing decision. Not saying I could have made my things right without getting sober from alcohol, but for me, that change needed to be made to get to this point.

## MOMENT #2: KELLY'S ADVICE

The COVID pandemic gave me a boatload of free time during the summer of 2020. With not much to do, I started to favor writing as a time filler. Big ideas began to preoccupy my mind as I questioned what in my life was worth writing about. Writing a book was something I really wanted to do, but I had no idea where to start. I lacked confidence and knew I would have to look outside of myself for some guidance. Asking for help is not one of my strengths. I've been afraid to seek assistance, fearful of appearing incompetent. Insecurities related to my intelligence have held me back for many years. To my surprise, something came over me, and I reached out (via email) to one of my favorite authors, Kelly McGonigal. Kelly is a health psychologist, lecturer at Stanford University, and author of many successful books. To my astonishment, Kelly not only responded but wrote an entire paragraph. I understand it might have been her run-of-the-mill advice, but to me it was riveting. It introduced me to a new perspective that I had never contemplated. Her advice played a crucial part in this book breaking ground. I am so grateful I put my pride away and reached out to somebody who's been where I'm trying to go. My advice to you guys is to seek knowledge, insight, and wisdom from somebody who's accomplished what you're trying to achieve. We all need a helping hand on the way to our ultimate destination.

## KELLY'S EMAIL

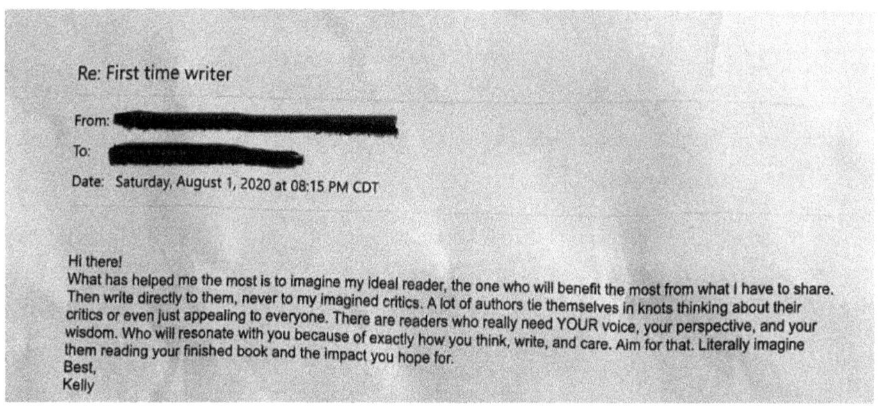

Re: First time writer

From:

To:

Date: Saturday, August 1, 2020 at 08:15 PM CDT

Hi there!
What has helped me the most is to imagine my ideal reader, the one who will benefit the most from what I have to share. Then write directly to them, never to my imagined critics. A lot of authors tie themselves in knots thinking about their critics or even just appealing to everyone. There are readers who really need YOUR voice, your perspective, and your wisdom. Who will resonate with you because of exactly how you think, write, and care. Aim for that. Literally imagine them reading your finished book and the impact you hope for.
Best,
Kelly

# ONE YEAR SOBER: DECEMBER 8, 2023

I sit before you today, typing this sentence about how today marks my 1st anniversary of being sober from alcohol. I can't believe that a year ago today, I consciously decided to abstain from alcohol altogether. It's hard to identify the main differences in my life now, but I honestly believe I am living the life intended for me. The outward transformation is obviously with weight loss, but the main transformation took place from within.

Abstaining from alcohol forced me to deal with my problems head-on. I could no longer use alcohol to distract, numb, or dissuade my thoughts or feelings. I had to develop healthy ways to express my thoughts and feelings while channeling my emotions positively. Abstaining from alcohol led me to start journaling my thoughts, prioritizing sleep, exercising daily, and strengthening my most intimate relationships.

One of the most significant changes I noticed when I stopped drinking alcohol, and the people around me can undoubtedly vouch for this, was a better mood. The days of having such drastic mood swings with the high highs and the low lows don't plague me as severely. Being sober has allowed me to keep a steadier state of mind that doesn't teeter as much. I show up every day with more balance. I still have days where I run on the low end, but I have healthier methods in place to wait out the passing fog.

The negative thoughts that once swamped my mind are starting to dry up. The decrease in negative thoughts has allowed my self-confidence to grow leaps and bounds. The further away I get from my last drink, the more growth I start to recognize. New doors continue to open, and possibilities seem endless, as I ride this wave of discovery. Getting sober has been a necessary decision for me to live life to my greatest potential and be the best version of myself for others. Before getting sober, I would have told you that my life purpose was to help others in any way that I could, but I would fail to acknowledge how I could help myself. I am pleased to see how much growth I have seen in the realm of self-love. Even for selfless individuals, it is okay to put yourself first.

# 'TWAS THE NIGHT BEFORE CHRISTMAS 2023: DECEMBER 24, 2023

Being the one consistent family member who is either attending or not attending family gatherings often leaves you out of the loop. Sure, you are part of the family, but can you truly build a sense of connection when you are only around part-time? It is hard, and maybe others who have separate families can relate to my thoughts on the matter. It's hard to explain, but you can literally be with one side of your family, try to connect with the other, and feel entirely rejected. Not rejected, just dismissed with a simple hello and bye—let's get back to our holiday celebration. I think that's why I have avoided being around for holidays, because in a way, I don't like the feeling of being the odd man out. As the saying goes, "out of sight, out of mind," and boy is that true.

I want more than anything to build my own family by getting married and having kids. I would like the consistency of having my wife and kids with me all the time. I can be grateful for having two loving families, but I can also want things to be different for my kids. I make a vow on this day, December 24, 2023, to always celebrate meaningful moments and holidays together until the kids reach 18. I will try my best to be present in my family members' lives and continue to attend holidays and trips when I can. I did feel a little rejected tonight, and that may be my sensitive nature, and I know my family meant no harm. It's just the way I perceived the call and how I felt, that's all.

No need to make a bigger deal of the situation. Time to move forward. Hang tight with me; I feel ready to go on a tangent.

I can be surrounded by several people and still feel lonely. Why do I feel so disconnected from people at times? And why am I so guarded? I don't let people in and keep people at arm's length—why do I do this? This may be a complete overreaction, and honestly, it doesn't even matter. All this chit-chat is beneficial because it gives me an outlet to express my thoughts without worrying about judging myself. To be frank with myself, I need to take a hard look in the mirror and see where I could be better. Could I do a better job of integrating myself?

Yes, I could. This may sound a little strange, but having a laptop and keyboard is my sanctuary. Sometimes you have to be your own shrink, and, in the end, you have to allow the shrink in you to enter your force field. I have covered a wide range of emotions in this journaling session, to the point that I have completely deviated from the original idea behind it.

That is okay, if that's the way things tend to go. I feel a little down, and I want to be alone for a bit. That's okay. I'll watch a movie or relax in my own comfort. Allow the time and space you need and let it pass.

## GRANDMA SHARON: MARCH 20, 2024

When I arrived at the hospital, I was warmly greeted by my grandfather and aunt. My grandma was awake and watching TV as I walked over to her bedside. She looked my way and gave a brief grin. She would respond when provoked, but she had the faintest whisper followed by nonsensical words. Occasionally, she would twitch her feet or reach for nothing in the air. Time must have been on my side that day because I got to see my grandma in a one-on-one capacity, and she got to know that I was there for her. Not long after I arrived, she became more restless, going in and out of sleep. For the remainder of the day and moving forward, when I was present, Grandma was unable to regain the level of alertness she had when I first arrived. Because of the decline, I felt incredibly blessed that I came when I did, and we got to have what would be our last encounter. That simple grin told me she had detected my presence. It felt really comforting to be surrounded by family, no matter how close we had been in previous years. We all came together to be there for Grandma on her end-of-life journey and set aside our individual differences. Seeing my grandpa light up with every arriving family member warmed my heart. Seeing all the family members dote on grandpa and support him let me know he wasn't alone.

Dear Grandma Sharon,

Will you thank God for having my book sent priority mail to heaven so you could read these words? I hope to hear you are free of all the pain and suffering you endured here on earth. I hope you felt the love I had for you when I came and saw you at the hospital. Thank you for treating me like one of your own. You didn't have to go out of your way to include my siblings and me in holiday celebrations and birthdays, but you did. It meant a lot to have your love and compassion as a bonus grandma. I will miss your hugs, warm vibes, and the feel of your soft cheek after kissing you. We didn't share the same blood, but that didn't impact the love you had for me. I love you, Grandma. See you again someday.

Love,
Bren

**MAKING A TOUGH PHONE CALL: JULY 7, 2024**

Yesterday was one of those days when I had to be the bad guy. Over a late-night phone call, I let my then-girlfriend know my heart was no longer invested in our relationship. In the month before this phone call, I began to have doubts about the relationship. Almost ten months in, and any semblance of a connection was MIA. I never truly reached a level of comfort that one should have at that stage in a relationship. At times, I felt like I was on a first date all over again, with the same uncertainty and anxiousness ever present. Before I made this phone call, I repeatedly rehearsed what I would say to portray my most sincere thoughts. This was one of the toughest phone calls I have made because of the respect and feelings I have for this girl.

We had a good relationship that included lunch dates, trips, and arcade game dates. We both had a strong sense of loyalty and trust, hard to find in today's world with all the temptations at our fingertips. We both shared an interest in food; her cooking it and me eating it. We really had some neat experiences and times together that I will never forget. This was a healthy and beneficial relationship that lacked one crucial thing: connection. I can only speak for myself, but the spark between us was dimly lit. Early on, I had hoped the connection piece would grow, but I've realized it's something you either have with someone or you don't. Because I cared for this girl, it hurt when I let her know I was no longer interested in pursuing a romantic relationship. I let it be known that I am open to and hopeful about remaining friends. Time will tell whether that comes true, but if it doesn't, I have no regrets about our time together. I got to experience love, learn new things, and travel with a cool girl. Sometimes relationships fizzle out with no one to blame, but you can still wish that person peace and happiness from a place of love. If I could tell her one last thing, I'd let her know that she had a part to play in my growth as a person and the writing of this book. For that, I will always be indebted to her.

## THE STRONGEST WAVE: JULY 13, 2024

In the last week, I have experienced a myriad of thoughts and ideations. Ideations of alcohol persist with each passing day. So far, I've resisted alcohol, but I can't say the same thing for other unhelpful desires. Last weekend, I went to the casino, and my daily sugar consumption has steadily increased, as have my negative thoughts. I've hit a rough patch, and this stretch will be the toughest to endure while staying sober. Without predicting the future, I know I'm riding the strongest wave as we speak. Now is the time for me to provide some context. As you just read, I broke up with my girlfriend a week ago, and in 19 days I'll be moving. Treading water during this transition period has tested me in every way, and will continue to do so. Writing will continue as I find ways to cope with change. Relying on my family and friends for support is something I have taken full advantage of.

Mom called me this morning to check on how I was doing, and that meant the world to me. I worked out this morning and went for a walk, which helped start my day on the right path. Having this time to reflect on the week and spending time doing things for myself has helped tremendously. I decided to tweak my diet starting today, and I look forward to the process of improving my health. Today has been a good day, and I can't wait for what lies ahead. Tomorrow is another day to improve, grow, reflect, plan, appreciate, and so on. Last week wasn't ideal, and I am making the necessary changes to support, expand, and strengthen my mind and my body.

## MOVING: AUGUST 6, 2024

Five days ago, I spent my first night in my new apartment. I feel like moving, in a way, hits the reset button on your psyche, and if you aren't ready for it, it will kick your butt. With so much unfamiliarity at times, I ask myself, "What are you doing?" or "Now what happens?" My newly cemented habits are still sticking, but now I'm doing them in a new place with a different set-up. In previous years, I would rely heavily on alcohol during that initial phase of a move. I would drink to calm my nerves when I saw the cluttered and disorganized living space. Everything in my living space has a designated place, and anything out of place is noticed immediately. The smartest decision I made during this move was to take an entire day off (since I moved in on a Wednesday) to unpack my belongings. On that day, I was able to close out some previous services, unpack, and make a list of things I still needed. No matter how prepared I am or how well I set myself up for success, I still feel inadequate. Do I miss my previous apartment? Is it starting to sink in that I'm single again? Do I need to drink when I move? I find myself spending more time looking for dating opportunities and becoming obsessed with it. My feelings toward myself should not change based on my location, but my actions are telling a different story. I don't have that strong sense of myself right now, and this writing session is a starting point for getting that back. I withstood the first barrage, but now it's time to lay the ground rules. I'll check back in a week to give y'all an update.

## MOVING (ONE WEEK IN): AUGUST 13, 2024

What a difference a week can make. Those feelings of uncertainty and doubt have slowly dissolved as the week has gone on. It took a little time, but this new apartment is starting to feel like home. I needed time to gain consistency and for my mind and body to adapt to their new environment. Allowing myself to take in all the latest and unfamiliar things without masking my feelings has made this transition much smoother. Last week, my pillar (stability) took some damage but ultimately withstood the storm. It seems silly now, and will seem even more ridiculous in the future, but I was feeling lost during the initial phase of this move.

Making any change can be hard, but sometimes we have to weather the storm. I had to get through the first week before my core self and foundation returned to the picture. All the self-development and growth I've made since giving up alcohol kicked in, and I feel like myself again. I am proud of myself for sticking to my stress management techniques and helpfully addressing my state of mind. Never let your environment dictate who you are. Easier said than done, but for some of us, it takes real fortitude and strength to be who we are in every circumstance.

## COMING HOME: SEPTEMBER 15, 2024

Once my lease is up, I'm packing my bags and moving back home. I've been fortunate to have two places I call home in my life, and one of them is Colorado. In 2016, I left Colorado and my family to go to school in Eastern Kansas. Had I been more patient, I could have attended a school in Colorado, but deep down, I wanted to get away. Over the years, I've had plenty of opportunities to move back to Colorado, and my Gran always assures me I have a place to stay until I get on my feet. The thought of returning home has crossed my mind, but the feelings I had when I last lived there keep creeping back. After this last trip to Colorado in late August of 2024, I started daydreaming about a possible return. I've arrived at the stage of my self-discovery where I question daily what is important to me. Right now, work is the main reason I reside in Southwest Kansas. Work is important, but at the end of the day, to many organizations, you are one of many, and they will replace you as quickly as they hired you. I also miss the outdoor adventures you have at your doorstep in Colorado and the little to no humidity. I want to see my family more regularly and be around for holiday get-togethers with the ones I grew up with. I want to spend more time with my Gran and be there at a moment's notice if she needs me. I'm not hiding who I am anymore, and I feel comfortable with myself. Moving back to Colorado in the Summer of 2025 will be another big life change that I look forward to.

## TAKING THE ROAD LESS TRAVELED: OCTOBER 22, 2024

Since moving to Kansas in the summer of 2016, I have lived alone and away from my family. I've hinted at this before, but moving away from family was fueled by a host of insecurities. I essentially wanted to hide who I really was at the time. I was a problematic drinker who felt like a complete failure. I wanted to get my degree and return home as a squeaky-clean professional. I wanted to come back home, secure, a girl by my side, drinking a non-issue, and ready to put that new degree to the test. I had it all planned out. I was going to use those two years away to get everything figured out. It sounded great in theory, but I never imagined my drinking issues getting worse. Living alone can create loneliness that, if not channeled correctly, can lead to poor coping mechanisms. I relied on poor coping mechanisms for years, while failing to make any strides within the sphere of personal development. Most areas of my life improved after giving up alcohol, and living alone was no exception. Instead of disconnecting from reality on weeknights or weekends, I was forced to be with myself. Luckily, I integrated some good time fillers (one of which I'm doing right now), and that made time alone much easier to manage. The more secure I've grown, the more okay I've felt living alone. I've lived alone all these years, but that didn't necessarily mean I've felt comfortable alone all these years. I do now, and this is the path I've chosen. There may be a time when I choose a different path, but for now, this will do. I'm in no rush to make any big changes in my life. Would I like to find a girl to date, of course. Would I like to eventually get married and have some kiddos running around, of course. It would be nice to come home every night to a family, but if that's not in the cards for me, I'll manage.

## WHY AM I NEVER THE SAME PERSON EVERY DAY? NOVEMBER 06, 2024

I envy people who show up as the same person every day. In the last two chapters of this book, you can identify my wavering thoughts a mile away. Some days I take a firm stance on decisions, and other days I feel like hiding in a corner when one is needed. To some degree, I have always been this way, and I think that's why I've had a hard time making good connections in my life. I know we as humans fluctuate in our moods, but I can't help but feel my case is a little more extreme. Some days I am bright-eyed, eager to engage in conversation, and other days I walk around on eggshells, hoping to be left alone. No question removing alcohol improved my mood swings, but it didn't eradicate them. On my list of issues, this sits low, but it still bothers me enough to write about. Do any of you guys feel this way about yourself? I know we all have our days, but I think I struggle to be consistent from day to day. More likely than not, I'll have to seek outside help with this topic. I'm aware of my inconsistencies, and I may never figure out why on my own.

We all have blind spots, and I'm okay saying I have my fair share, too. To get the clarity and answers I want, I'll need to seek guidance. Some may view this as a character flaw, but I see it as an area for improvement. I know many (I've been guilty myself in the past) like to label anyone who seeks psychological or psychiatric help as a head case, but I'm not here for that. Instead, let's applaud those seeking professional help. I haven't mentioned this yet, but now seems like the right time to state that I've gone in for counseling myself.

I hit a rough patch in 2018, and someone recommended that I go in for counseling. I was hesitant at first because of my perceptions of counseling, but I decided to give it a try. I didn't think I met the requirements, but I was wise enough to look past that. When I walked through the front door for my first session, I realized that people from all walks of life came in for counseling. I ended up going for four sessions, and the insight I gained was very valuable to me. It was a productive outlet for me, and a lot of darkness came to light during those sessions. Living in a high emotional state meant I wasn't seeing the whole picture. Many things were outside my periphery, but I left each counseling session looking through a clearer lens on life. I made a life change in 2019 that was very beneficial for my well-being, and I don't know if I would have made it had I not gone for counseling. Based on everything I've just said, it only seems right that we meet again for counseling in the future.

## TWO YEARS SOBER: DECEMBER 09, 2024

Yesterday marked two years of sobriety, and I chose to make my first public declaration. Ordinarily, I would have written on the day of my soberversary, but I wanted to soak up all the thoughts and feelings I had surrounding my two years of sobriety. While I chose not to write, I instead decided to share my sober story on social media via Facebook and Instagram. The largest audience I currently have at my disposal is my Facebook friends and Instagram followers. Sharing my story via social media is something that I've been meticulously planning for months now. I've kicked around how I would tell my story until I found a method that stuck. December 8, 2024, has been circled on my calendar since summertime, and now that day is finally here. I went to the gym to push some iron around and, more importantly, calm my nerves. Sharing my story makes me uncomfortable because of my worrisome mind. I retreated to my long-established way of thinking, and that obviously gets me nowhere. I get these invasive thoughts about people scoffing at my post and not giving me the approval I think I need. Yesterday, when the clock struck 08:00 am Central Time, it was time to step up to the plate. I had to keep my true intention for sharing my story in mind and be okay with where I stood. I dealt with some early jitters as I wrote my story, and by the time I hit the post button, I was holding firm. For the first time publicly, I shared my struggles with alcohol, areas of self-growth, advice on making a change, and stated my intentions of reintroducing alcohol into my life. This is something I really wanted to do, and I was pleased to make it happen. Now I can reflect on my two years of sobriety.

It doesn't seem possible that I have been sober for two years. Life really goes by in the blink of an eye, and moments like this remind you to appreciate every day. I'm appreciative of where I am in life. On the outside, not much has changed in terms of external success (not yet, at least), but internally, I have more purpose and drive than at any point in my life. In year 1 of my sobriety, I took in what it felt like to live a sober life. My main goal was to stay sober, but I replaced alcohol with other numbing vices.

In year 1, I was living a sober life, but in year 2, I started living my life. I established some solid routines and found some inspiration to learn. I wanted to learn more about myself and work on the areas I felt I was lacking. I gained more clarity on what I want in life and who I want to be. Along those lines, I started to develop a backbone when it came to standing up to that inner voice. In year two of sobriety, I started pushing my comfort zone and exploring this new me.

My self-belief grew minute by minute, and my destiny became set in stone. This will be the last rendition of my yearly soberversary, as I've chosen to reintroduce alcohol, but I know I can always go back and read this to see how far I've come.

I want to elaborate on why I decided (not that I have to) to reintroduce alcohol. I know what a lot of you may be thinking: if you've made all this growth sober, why in the hell would you go back to drinking? Trust me, I've asked myself that same question. For me, I've arrived at the point where I feel comfortable with who I am. My drinking identity is a shell of its former self, and I've hit the reset button. Who I am as a person does not correlate to alcohol. Experiencing life for two years without alcohol showed me I don't need it for any life circumstance. Alcohol was a problem because of the decisions I made. Alcohol itself, when handled responsibly, is not the culprit. In the past, I blamed alcohol for my behavior, for overindulging, for blacking out, for shitty hangovers, and for creating feelings of emptiness.

I decided to use alcohol as a coping mechanism. I relied on alcohol to give me confidence and courage when I lacked it on my own. I'll be honest, I want the challenge of reintroducing alcohol. I know in the back of my mind, the side of my mind, and the front of my mind, that this idea could go haywire if I don't approach it the right way. Something about that rush has made me ready to sink my teeth into this next challenge. It's time to button my chin strap and test all the hard work I've put in.

# SECTION II-B: ALCOHOL REINTRODUCTION—FIRST SIX MONTHS

## OKLAHOMA TRIP DECEMBER 17, 2024

This Oklahoma trip has been carefully planned for months, and I say carefully because I wanted to find an ideal place to have my first sip of alcohol after two years. I wanted to visit the state of Oklahoma for a variety of reasons, but at the end of the day, this trip would be remembered for my reintroduction to alcohol (or so I thought). Meeting the family member of an American Icon was not something I expected to happen. Before I let the cat out of the bag, let's start at the beginning.

I hit the road for Oklahoma on the morning of December 13, 2024, but the basis of this trip was established in the summer of 2024. In recent years, some of Oklahoma's dark history has been brought to light through documentaries and movies. I felt so inclined by many of these stories that I wanted to experience them for myself. These historical sites and stories gave me a real reason to visit Northeast Oklahoma, all while knowing, deep inside, that I was planning this trip around my two-year sobriety date. I wanted to experience a new environment and reintroduce alcohol on my own terms. This was something I needed to do for myself and by myself.

Day one of the trip centered on my visits to the Osage Nation Museum in Pawhuska, Oklahoma, and the Jim Thorpe House in Yale, Oklahoma. This was an area full of Native American culture and pride, and it was well on display during my drive in. After visiting the Osage Nation Museum, I set out to see where the legendary Native American figure Jim Thorpe once lived. I noticed on the Jim Thorpe House website months earlier that you could walk through the house, but I didn't know if it was one of those shifting situations where it was only open certain times of the year or could be closed due to renovations. I really had my mind set on driving by the house, maybe taking a couple of pictures, and getting back on the road.

As I arrived at the house, I noticed it had a small parking area in front, and I was the only car that filled it. I got out of the car to take some pictures and realized there were lights on inside the house. I approached the door and slowly opened it while shouting, "Is anyone home?" My shout met with complete silence, and not a human being was in sight. I decided, well, I'm in the house that Jim Thorpe once lived in—I might as well look around. The home was neatly organized, with photos of Jim Thorpe and his family, as well as award plaques and achievements scattered throughout. Not long after I started nosing around, I heard a welcoming voice coming from the back of the house.

A woman entered the living room and formally welcomed me to the Jim Thorpe House. She thanked me for coming, introduced herself as Anita, and then started showing me around the home. Not that I wasn't engaged or paying attention, but a few minutes into our interaction, Anita piqued my curiosity when she mentioned, in a lackadaisical way, that she was a descendant of Jim Thorpe. My antennas were up as my conversation with Anita took a turn for the better. Not that it was bad by any means, but as she started sharing stories about (what I learned was) her grandfather, Jim Thorpe, our conversation became significantly more personal. Hearing her speak so glowingly of her grandfather, without ever having met him, made me reflect on my own late grandfather. For roughly thirty minutes, Anita and I were just two people speaking about our grandfathers, and it was such a memorable experience.

I shared my past with alcohol and my plan for reintroducing alcohol during this trip to Oklahoma. Before I left, I awkwardly took a picture with Anita inside the house. As I left the Jim Thorpe Home, I posted on Facebook to share the excitement I was feeling at the time with others. Day one in Oklahoma was a resounding success.

I had to open my travel journal to refresh my memory (I'm writing this section at a much later time) on how day two went on my trip to Oklahoma. The morning began with a visit to the historic Greenwood district in downtown Tulsa. I won't get into all the details surrounding the Tulsa Massacre of 1921, but I will encourage you to look it up on your own time. What I want you to know right now is that a senseless tragedy took place in the predominantly black district of Greenwood, in the heart of Tulsa. Seeing where all the local establishments and businesses (that were burned to the ground) once stood had a powerful effect on me. I had so much sympathy and anger running through my veins when I took in this unforgettable scene. The devastation that was inflicted on an entire community could have been the end of the story, but it wasn't. The people of the Greenwood district regained their bearings, rebuilt their neighborhood, and stood unwavering in their commitment to each other and their neighborhood. After grabbing some lunch at Shawkat's Mediterranean restaurant, I headed for Muskogee. In Muskogee, I visited the Three Rivers Museum (mainly to see a life-like mannequin of Bass Reaves) and then stopped at Muskogee War Memorial Park. The main attraction at the park was the USS Batfish, a World War II submarine that was active and sank many enemy ships.

It was around 2:30 p.m., and I had an hour ride back to Tulsa, and that's when the thoughts of alcohol started to prey on my mind. I got to my hotel room and devoured some cookies I bought from a local bakery. I watched some basketball for about an hour, but really, I was stalling. I was wary about going to the bar across the street. I no longer craved alcohol, and I was unsure how things would unfold once I had that first sip. Would I resort to my old ways? Would I have wasted two years of my life working on myself and my underlying issues, only for it to all be for naught? Nobody was holding a gun to my head and making me drink alcohol. I knew my life had changed for the better when I made that decision two years ago, and I kept telling myself, if it doesn't work out, I can always reclaim my sobriety.

Eventually, I summoned the courage to walk to the bar across the street. I stayed in the bar for about two hours, had some conversations, most notably with a man from Uganda, and enjoyed three Blue Moons. I drank these beers on my terms, and I decided I had enough (for now). I felt in control of my decisions, and I liked how I handled that initial introduction. After resting in my hotel room for about two hours, I decided to take an Uber to a brewery for some food and drinks. Apparently, I wasn't done drinking for the day, so I had two more beers with my dinner, Ubered back home, and called it a night.

The next morning, I woke up and got on the road back to Kansas. I was on a self-belief high the entire ride home. I felt so empowered by executing the plan I had set for myself when it came to alcohol. I missed the taste of cold beer, and I genuinely enjoy a beer on a hot summer day or after a long day of work. I had pushed myself to be out there more, in terms of living life. I felt so held back from living life due to fear, self-doubt, and insecurities related to all my problems. I handcuffed myself for so long that it felt good to do the things I revel in without any second thoughts. I checked off a lot of personal boxes during this trip. I enjoy traveling and visiting places I find interesting, check. I enjoy trying different cuisines—check. I'm starting to enjoy meeting new people with different backgrounds, check. I enjoy the taste of beer now and then, check. I enjoy my own presence, check, the most important check of all.

A few days after I got back home, I felt compelled to write to Anita Thorpe. The impact of our interaction didn't fully hit me until I absorbed the moment a few days later. I appreciated how she made me feel by speaking of and honoring her grandfather, Jim Thorpe. I also wrote to Anita to get her blessing. I told her about this book (she was the first person I told), and I wanted her permission to speak about the moment she and I shared in the Jim Thorpe House. She wrote me back and gave me the permission I was looking for; otherwise, this chapter would look desolate. Visiting the Jim Thorpe House and speaking with Anita Thorpe was the highlight of my trip to Oklahoma. If you're ever in Northeast Oklahoma or feel like making a trip, visit the Jim Thorpe House in Yale, Oklahoma.

# ANITA THORPE'S RESPONSE

1/3/25, 2:41 PM Yahoo Mail - Thank you

Thank you

From: Anita Thorpe [redacted]

To: brengreg1990@yahoo.com

Date: Friday, January 3, 2025 at 11:00 AM CST

Good morning,

I'm at the Yale home this morning and it was such a nice surprise to open up your letter.

Your words were just what I needed hear at the beginning of this new year.

I'd love to be included in your book and hope it inspire readers as you have inspired me today.

Much respect to you and your family, may you have a blessed year.

Anita

Sent from my iPhone

# GOING FOR A TEST RUN IN NEW MEXICO: MARCH 20, 2025

For this trip, my soul was telling me to travel westbound. It turned out that the Southwest Chief train went through Garden City and went all the way to Los Angeles. For future reference or anyone interested, the same train heading eastbound goes to Chicago. As luck would have it, a train destined for the big cities meanders its way through a small town on the southwest Kansas plains. Traveling by train to a place I've never been to sounds like a fun voyage, in theory. I say in theory because my past self would have been too scared of all the unknowns.

I settled on Albuquerque, because other than driving through a tiny sliver of the Northwest part of the state, I had never experienced New Mexico. Round-trip tickets cost me a total of $70, and when you get a bargain like that, you can't let it go to waste. A few weeks later, I booked my hotel room for three nights, and the trip was set. Not having to drive also eliminated the possibility of my drinking and driving. I've changed my drinking ways, but I still want to set myself up for success when it comes to alcohol because I know deep down what I'm capable of. Taking control out of my hands is of the utmost importance to me. The morning of March 13, 2025, came way too early as I woke up at 4:15 a.m. to get ready for my 5:45 a.m. train departure to Albuquerque. Eleven hours later, I stepped foot off the train, and the moment of truth arrived.

Three days later, and I had grown in ways I didn't think about until I was on the train back to Kansas. Before I get to the nitty-gritty of this trip, I do want to talk about the train experience. Part of me looked forward to having around eleven hours (twelve hours on the way back) of idle time to learn, reflect, create, and take in the landscape. I read an entire book, listened to a podcast and music, generated ideas, and reflected on my trip, all during the train ride back. I could hardly get comfortable in the seats, but luckily, I wasn't seeking comfort or sleep. I had to endure the occasional loud passenger, crying baby, or overbearing train attendant, but that's what I signed up for.

Going out to New Mexico and living life pushed me towards discomfort. Every time I encountered a stranger in the hotel, a restaurant, a bar, a shop, or in my Uber, I made a conscious decision to spread kindness and love with a vibrant tone. I wanted to reflect who I truly was and work through my insecurities and doubts. I was proud of how I connected and conversed with strangers. I had some memorable interactions from this trip that I plan to carry with me as a badge of honor. I pushed myself towards what has traditionally been uncomfortable for me. I even carried out my daily routines on vacation, which reminded me that I can continue them even in an unfamiliar environment. That reinforced that my routines, thoughts, and beliefs come from within and can be performed in any external environment. I also felt inspired by the culture and traditions of New Mexico. Seeing the powerful displays of art and authenticity that the people in the state have inspires me to pour my whole self into everything I do.

The Albuquerque Museum has an exhibit honoring the people of New Mexico. They proclaim the people of New Mexico are resourceful, innovative, courageous, and spirited. In this same exhibit, they have an interactive module where you can record (via video) your story and share an experience where you displayed one of the four adjectives I spoke of. I went into the module and hit the record button, but halfway through, I stopped and deleted it. I wasn't ready to share my story, but trust me, I'm getting closer.

# MOMENT #3: LITTLE RAVEN

A few years back, my mom gifted me a picture frame that holds what you see on the previous page—the origin of my name. Growing up, I was not fond of the name "Brennen." For starters, people were constantly mispronouncing or misspelling it, but I suppose that comes with the territory when you have a unique name. Looking back, I feel the disdain I had for my name stemmed from not liking who I was. With time, I've slowly come around to the idea that my name fits me, and the origin of my name reflects that. The spelling of my name varies slightly, but it translates to Little Raven. The raven is revered for its wisdom and prophecy, and I take on the onus to live by those traits.

P.S. I'm sorry, Mom, there was a time when I didn't like my name. I want to thank you for jazzing up my name and picking a name that would one day suit me.

I AM BRENNEN "BREN" "LITTLE RAVEN" GREGORY

## SIMPLE GESTURES MATTER: MARCH 29, 2025

On Friday, March 28, 2025, I was walking home after a long week. The week felt so grueling because of all the continuing education I had to get done before the end of the month.

As an Occupational Therapy practitioner, you must complete forty hours of AOTA-approved classes or literature every two years. I usually have my forty hours wrapped up months before the deadline, but the reason I didn't isn't important, and I'm getting away from the point of this story. As I was de-stressing on my lumbering stroll home, a car came up alongside me (which isn't anything new, as I've been offered a ride a few times now). He was a former patient of mine who offered me a ride home. I thanked him for the offer, but declined. We caught up for a minute with the typical chitchat. As the conversation neared an end, we started to go our separate ways, but before he drove off, he said one last thing. He said, "I kind of figured you would decline my offer for a ride, but I saw you, and I wanted to come say hi." As we diverged, that last sentence stayed with me: "I wanted to come say hi." Without delay, my stressful thoughts from moments earlier melted away, and I felt immense gratitude.

We get so caught up in our own heads at times and so narrow-minded that we forget to see and appreciate the little things. I felt extremely cared about, and the fact that someone took time out of their day to do something as simple as say hi makes my eyes well up as I write this. It was a typical interaction that most of us experience countless times a day, but then again, it wasn't. I was at my wits' end for the day, but I knew right away this wasn't some middling interaction.

A higher power set up the scene for him and me to have that interaction, and I needed to hear those words at that exact time to gain the perspective I needed. That simple gesture shifted the complexion I was carrying at the time and set the tone for how I start my Saturday morning, with gratitude. I needed his thoughtfulness and compassion to lift me out of my self-created misery. I know I've been a beacon of hope for others, but now I'm seeing how others are propping me up and inspiring me with simple gestures that lead to timely impact. Never discount the importance you bring to this world. What happened yesterday reminded me of another time when someone made my day.

## MOMENT #4: DON'T DISCOUNT THE IMPORTANCE OF A FIRST IMPRESSION

I had a visceral reaction when I heard the news of a stranger passing. I was moved to tears because of what this man meant to me during our only interaction. Honestly, I don't ever cry, but this hit me differently.

In May 2020, I was still learning the ropes of my new job in Sioux City, Iowa. It can be a steep learning process with an ever-changing schedule. While working on various units is good for creating a well-balanced, diverse therapist, it can feel overwhelming at first. Identifying the rooms, the floors, the specific nurses, doing chart reviews, and knowing where all the devices and supplies are can be a lot at first.

On this specific day, I remember feeling drained and ready for the day to be over. I remember looking around for the nurse assigned to my next patient's room. I soon approached a large man who looked Native American and thought to myself, there's no way he's a nurse. This man with lips tattooed on his neck didn't fit the mold. I asked if he was the nurse for a specific room number, and he confirmed he was. I asked him some more questions about the patient, and he answered my initial questions, but he didn't stop there. He went on to provide me with more information about the patient. It was so helpful to gain that extra insight before I saw my patient.

My whole attitude changed because I sensed how genuinely interested in their progress he was and how genuine he was to me. I was new to the city, and it felt like it was me against the world at times. I felt like an outsider, but after this encounter, I felt accepted. He had such a calming demeanor in such a hectic environment, and I fed off that energy. In that moment, I was able to exhale. He actually stopped in the middle of what he was doing and gave me his full, undivided attention during our conversation.

To find someone who is that respectful and patient in this line of work is rare. During my session, I remember leaving the patient's room to look for a washcloth, and there he was again, answering my question. This time, he actually walked me to the room where I could find the linens, instead of just telling me where the room was. He even asked for an update on how the patient was doing in therapy. I remember walking to my car after my shift and thinking that guy would make a good friend.

The next time I saw him, he was walking a patient with a smile, showing what kind of person he was. Later, I heard about his tragic death in a car accident. When I reflected on his passing, I couldn't help but cry. I remembered that day and how much he helped me. My first impression of him is all I will ever know—though I didn't know his personal life, I sensed his compassion, sincerity, patience, care, respect, and the positive impact he made from just one brief encounter. The message here is to remember that first impressions can leave a lasting mark.

Showing kindness, compassion, and thoughtfulness, even during tough times, won't go unnoticed. I will always remember how Tyler James Big Bow influenced me. Rest peacefully, big fella.

# TYLER JAMES BIG BOW

## DWELLING IN QUANDARY: APRIL 9, 2025

I'm undecided on how to proceed with publishing my book. I'm finishing up last-minute topics and thinking about the next steps. I want the book to reflect my true self and showcase my creativity, leaning towards self-publishing. However, I also want to reach a broad audience, which suggests traditional publishing might be better, despite less control over the final product. Self-publishing lets me realize my vision, but requires me to handle marketing.

There are pros and cons on each side, and I must figure out what's more important to me. I continually revisit the words that are first spoken in "The Climb Back," by J. Cole: "Are you doing this work to facilitate growth or to become famous? Which is more important: getting or letting go?" The quote in the song comes from an automated voice, which led me to believe it didn't come from J. Cole himself. My curiosity vaulted me into action this morning as I tracked down the source of this quote. It didn't take long for me to find a more complete quote that came from a book. From *The Tao of Leadership: Lao Tzu's Tao Te Ching Adapted for a New Age* by John Heider, came the words below.

> Are you doing this work to facilitate growth or to become famous?
> Which is more important: acquiring more possessions or becoming more conscious?
> Which works better: getting or letting go?

Fragments of the quotes have been rooted in my head since I first heard this song a few years ago. I go back and forth on which is more important: facilitating growth or becoming famous. I have a general idea of how I want to move forward, but it's so fluid. I started this writing session off, thinking I might find the clarity I need by weighing my options, but I'm still questioning things. I'm learning to accept that I don't always have the answers right now, but I don't need to. No decision needs to be made today, and rushing ahead prohibits me from soaking up this once-in-a-lifetime experience. The nearing of this book is making me anxious about my next steps, and that's okay. I will appreciate the art of writing and stay in the moment. My time will come soon, and I'll cross that bridge when I come to it. Deal in the present, my friends.

## MY LETTER TO SOUTHWEST KS: APRIL 15, 2025

Dear Southwest Kansas,

I've pushed off writing to you for long enough. This will unequivocally be the toughest entry I have to write. I came to you back in the summer of 2018 as a young man trying to establish himself in a new line of work, in a foreign place. You took me in from the day I arrived on July 1st, 2018, and kept me. I was still wet behind the ears in several areas, and I never imagined still being here all these years later. In July of this year, it will be seven years since I've called you home. I won't make it for eight years, but I'll talk about that at the end. In the seven years I've been here, I ran away twice, in search of something, only to come back with my tail between my legs. Something didn't feel right when I left you, and coming back always lifted my spirit. You brought me comfort, a sense of belonging, and familiarity. I gravitated to you because of the people in this area. I differ from most people in this area in terms of interests or values, but where we connect is on a human level—things like mutual respect, compassion, and thoughtfulness.

I love the melting pot of southwest Kansas and all the culture that's on display here. I admire the commitment the people of this area have to their family first and foremost, and to the community. As an outsider, you accepted me without judgment. There were some rotten apples out there (just like anywhere), but for the most part, I was welcomed with open arms. I needed you to gather my bearings, to hone my craft, to get away from the chatter, and to practice solitude. You provided ideal conditions for me to flourish as a worker and, more importantly, as a human being. When I didn't know who I was or what I wanted to do with my life, you provided me a place to tie down my anchor. I'm not the man I am today if I had never moved to southwest Kansas. In the seven years I've been here, I've grown more as a person than in my previous 28 years combined. Unfortunately, the time has come for me to spread my wings and pursue other passions I have in life. Although my time here has come to an end, I am forever grateful. Thank you, Southwest Kansas.

Love always,
Bren

## STILL A WORK IN PROGRESS: MAY 7, 2025

Let me set the stage for you: I had a job interview earlier in the day that went well. I was offered a job that included a $5 raise, accepted it, and spent the evening in St. Joseph (St. Joe's), Missouri, with my mom and stepdad. It's easy to see why I felt elated and ready to celebrate. After finishing my job interview and before Mom arrived, I went to a bar in downtown St. Joe's. That's where my drinking adventures started, as I enjoyed two sour beers. Once mom arrived in town, I made my way over to the Hampton Inn. It was late afternoon, and we had a little time to kill before we made dinner plans. We decided to hit up the downtown. Tim drove, and my driving excursions were discontinued for the day. We had a few drinks and then went to dinner. After dinner, we went back to the hotel. It was around 8:30–9:00 p.m., and I was (A) wanting to watch the NBA playoffs and (B) wanting to drink more beer.

I Ubered to a bar & grill (which might become my go-to spot for watching sporting events) to watch the rest of the basketball game. After the game, I decided to Uber to BDubs. The answer to the question you're asking yourself right now is, yes, I kept the beers coming on this momentous night. I met some guys at BDubs, and we kept the party going. I tagged along as we went to another bar before making our way back to one of the guys' houses. During these explorations, I had to make some decisions. At that other bar, one of the guys ordered a round of shots, and without hesitation, I politely declined.

As I prepared myself for the typical peer-pressure statements, the bartender offered words of admiration. My decision was already fixed, but I appreciated that he admired my stance. I told the group of strangers that I stick to beer and stay away from the hard stuff. I took a step back from the bar and watched as they touched shot glasses and tipped one back. Even in my intoxicated state, I stayed away from the things that could really turn my night upside down. Over the course of the rest of the night, I was offered another substance entirely, which I again declined. I was sticking to my guns no matter what, and that night was an affirmation of that. The hardest thing I had to control that night was my bladder. I could barely go fifteen minutes without having to empty my bladder, and with some immediacy, might I add. Now, did I drink more than I would like to? Yes. I know this because, as I was getting a ride back to the hotel, things started to get fuzzy. My recollection was grainy in those moments, and that's the area I want to stay out of.

I minimized my risk of a bad outcome that night through the decisions I made, but I wasn't perfect. Nevertheless, you never know how you'll respond unless you're put in those make-or-break situations. I must be careful. I know I could lose my footing on this slippery slope. Up until this point, I had tested the waters of alcohol by sticking a toe in here or there. This past weekend, I jumped in the water, yelling "cannonball," and I still made it out of the water relatively unscathed. From this experience, I can collect data, examine it, and adjust accordingly.

# 6 MONTHS IN: JUNE 9, 2025

Today marks six months since I reintroduced alcohol into my life, and I'm still standing. In all seriousness, alcohol plays such a small role in my life now, and I'm grateful for that. You recently read about one of my nights where I drank in excess, but on a day-to-day basis, alcohol doesn't haunt my thoughts like it did in the past. Having specific parameters involving alcohol has served me well so far, and I'll continue to make revisions if deemed necessary. Having certain non-negotiables needs to be at the center of the table if I choose to drink alcohol. I'm going to stop saying the word alcohol, because the only thing I'm drinking is beer. Obviously, beer contains alcohol, but I'm fixated on staying away from the hard stuff, hard alcohol. I want to reinforce to myself that my hard alcohol days are long behind me. It doesn't hurt to continually hammer in that thought, so it doesn't escape my thick skull. These six months have been, and will continue to be, an experimental period for me when it comes to drinking beer. Reintroducing beer back in my life has led me to take more risks and address my fears.

I've noticed since the beginning of the year that I've really put myself out there to learn more about myself. At work, I've made myself available to attend more meetings and speak on behalf of the therapy department. Situations that usually make me anxious and uncomfortable are becoming more tolerable with repetition. I am voluntarily putting myself in awkward positions because I want to grow and become a leader. In return, I've gained more confidence, and I feel the growing admiration people have for me. I don't mean for this to come off as egotistical, but I'm starting to sense the impact I'm having on others. The ball doesn't stop at work; on social media, I've made my presence felt by sharing examples of growth and resilience I've demonstrated, with the intention of inspiring others. My self-belief continues to grow as I reinforce my vision and take on a daily challenge. One thing I started doing this past weekend is doing something I don't intrinsically want to do every day. I don't always want to exercise, read, write, take on a new task, make a phone call, or eat clean, but 1 time a day I strive to make myself do it anyways. I'll expand on this later in the book, but overcoming a challenge builds perseverance and that self-belief muscle. Man, I like where I'm at in life—not in my physical location per se, but in my mindset.

I'm living life on my terms, and I'm still finding what quenches my thirst for life. I'm on that Maximus Decimus Meridius (main character from the movie *Gladiator*) in the colosseum-type energy. Ready to take on all challenges and give it my all. Some days I won't have it, but it doesn't mean I won't later. The growth mindset is real to me, and I'm all in on growing it. I have a busy summer ahead of me that will involve many intricacies and unknowns. I've been building towards this moment, and I'm ready to keep this growth training rolling!

## A LETTER TO MY YOUNGER SELF: JUNE 28, 2025

Many of us would love the opportunity to write to our younger self, but would the younger you be willing to listen to the present you? Would the younger you shun or scold you for trying to "big bro" them? Nobody likes being told what to do, and until now, I've never questioned how the younger me would take advice from present me. It's easy to see where you went wrong in life when hindsight is 20/20. If I were to write a letter to the younger me, I think I would start from a place of love. I would remind young Bren that he is loved. What's the first thing you would say to the younger you? While you sit with that thought for a second, I'm going to write to the younger me.

Dear Bren,

It's the year 2025, and as I write this, I'm less than a week away from turning thirty-five years old. Let's not waste any time. The first thing I want you to know is that I love you. Many people love and care for you in this world. I know at times you have struggled to see how loved you are, and I'm culpable for seeing things through a muddied lens. Before I go any further, I want you to know I'm not trying to attack who you are or make you feel less than; instead, I want you to be present and take this all in. My words come from a place of love, and I want you to roll with the punches. As I said earlier, I'm soon to be thirty-five, and I'm still discovering who I am and what I truly want in life. I hope that last sentence doesn't scare you, but I don't want to lie to you and pretend everything is all gravy.

I want you to get a head start on learning who you are. Start the process of breaking down who you are as a person—those areas you excel in (you have many; I know what you're thinking right now) and those that need work. I need you to block out all the noise and focus on you. What things are you passionate about?

Not what things you think other people want you to do, but what things you enjoy. You are young, and I understand we want to be liked, and we seek the approval of others, but that can have devastating consequences. I want you to develop yourself. I'll say this, I'd rather be hated for being who I really am than to be loved for being someone who I think I should be. I realized after writing that last sentence that Kurt Cobain of Nirvana had a similar quote. Do you remember listening to the Nirvana album *Nevermind* on road trips with Dad when you were younger? You'll catch back on to Nirvana in the future, maybe sooner than later.

That quest for perfection you're after isn't attainable. Sit with your imperfections and understand you're going to make mistakes. That's life. I hope I'm not overwhelming you with all this information. Give yourself some time to unravel everything. Keep this letter with you and go back to it as many times as you need to. That reminds me: I want you to hear me out, but don't be afraid to enlist help from others. I know you don't want to show your struggle and keep up a certain appearance, but how's that working for you? It can be scary to put yourself out there, but trust me, there are people you can talk to and who won't judge you. I want you to know that things don't always have to be the same way, and you are capable of growth, Bren! On a similar note, in the future, you are going to make a big commitment to change, and that's all I'll say. I am by no means a finished product, but I have grown by leaps and bounds. Every day is a battle in fighting the old, and some days I lose that battle. More often than not, I find a way to grow and evolve. Keeping a growth mindset has been imperative to my development, and I never stray far from that perspective.

You can find meaning every day, whether it's a good or a bad day. Be careful with labeling things as good or bad, positive or negative, etc. Talk to yourself with kindness, as you would anyone else. Showing others kindness comes easily to you; now show yourself that same grace. Stay in the present, Bren. We miss so many things in the present when we ruminate over the past or wish for good fortune in the future. You only have control in the present moment; we can't change the past or predict the future. However, the action you take in the present moment can lead to the future you want.

Never let anyone or anything deviate you from your destiny. That's easy to say and so much harder to execute; therein lies the beauty of challenge. Life is about doing challenging things, making mistakes, failing, and still showing up. Build up your self-belief to a point where it can't be disturbed by any outside influence. We've been in the low-confidence category for years now, and to change that, we have to keep the promises we make to ourselves. Hold yourself accountable, Bren. Nobody is coming to save you; you need to save yourself. I want you to get to the point where you are borderline, no, actually, you are delusional about your abilities and desires. It's only delusional until you make it happen, then it becomes reality. We've been on the other side of the spectrum for so long, I want you shooting for the moon. We all have dreams and aspirations in life that, for whatever reason, fall by the wayside, but that one dream can't. At some point in life, you will be guided to your greater purpose, and you'll know what I'm talking about when you experience it. When that time comes, be ready to take the reins and lead the way for others to follow. Everything you're looking for is already inside of you; you just have to learn how to access it. I'm currently working on a big project, and let's just say you are destined for great things!

Love,

Bren

# MY BIRTHDAY MEANS VERY LITTLE WITHOUT OTHERS: JULY 2, 2025

Yesterday was my 35$^{th}$ birthday, and I had some things to share, but I allowed myself a moment to think. I want my thoughts to come off as clear and concise, but who are we kidding? That's not really my style. Anyway, I usually shrink on days like yesterday, but instead, I had a birthday revelation. In the past, birthdays reminded me of how unaccomplished I felt in life. Another year comes and goes, and I still feel as worthless as I did the year before. Those sorts of thoughts inundated my consciousness for years. I typically counted the hours, minutes, and seconds on that day, hoping time would speed up. Yesterday morning, I realized I was going to embrace my birthday and switched up my mindset. My birthday is a day for people in my life to shower me with love and appreciation. Sure, we shouldn't have a set day every year where we acknowledge someone we love or care about, but that's the way it is. Who am I to deny others the opportunity to celebrate me? That feels like a selfish act to me. I am worthy of the love and admiration I receive from others. My birthday means nothing without the people in my life. On this day, they bring me love, belonging, acceptance, connection, and kinship. Your birthday also shows who genuinely cares about you as a human being, and it's evident in people's actions—or lack thereof.

Open yourself up to be loved and accepted. If people show up for you in life, give them that same energy. I used to get upset when I called people on their birthdays, and they didn't return the favor. They might have written on my Facebook page or texted me, but it felt less than because it wasn't what I did. I stuck out my neck the furthest for people, and it wasn't always reciprocated. I need to correct myself, because I've also been the person who doesn't return the favor. I don't want this to come off as if I'm a saint all the time. I need to be educated on some things, and I think it's time to insert a quote to help me (and possibly you) realize some things. I've heard quotes of a similar variety before, but this one hit me right between the eyes. "Love is doing a kindness for someone else, not expecting to receive anything in return" (Reynard).

I was looking for transactional gestures in my relationships; what I do for you, I expect in return. I was missing the boat, and I can admit that now. My intentions now feel tainted, and I can honestly say many of my actions didn't come from a place of genuine love. Acts of love can take many forms, and everyone expresses that love in different ways. No act of love is less than or better than anyone else; it's simply an act of love. We constantly want the same in return—or more—but let's accept love in any form. Unfortunately, some people in this world experience very little love, and they would die to experience the kind of love many of us receive regularly. I want to leave you with three concepts from this chapter.

Be willing to be loved and celebrated by others.

Love hard, not looking for anything in return.

Acts of love come in all shapes and sizes; no act is better or worse.

## PINCH ME, I MUST BE DREAMING: JULY 22, 2025

I'm on the cusp of finishing this book, and it doesn't seem real. I hope this isn't one of those situations where anticipation kills the actual experience, but I can't contain my jubilation. Wavering thoughts no longer plague me, and this book finally feels imminent. This budding self-belief has been primed for moments like this, and I refuse to let anything escape my grasp. Hang tight, I'm sure you can tell by how this chapter is starting that I'm going to boast a little. I've accomplished what I set out to do: write a book. The next step is getting the book into the hands of the readers who are meant to read it, and anything after that is a bonus. I'm in the eleventh hour, and I can't help but feel grateful for this whole process. I'm in full embrace mode, as I now add the finishing touches and final edits to this book. This isn't glamorous work, but I'm finding motivation in the tediousness of it all. This chapter didn't have much of a concept; I just wanted to jot down some final thoughts that would one day put a smile on my face. Someday down the road, I can read this page and feel proud of what I accomplished. I know it seems like we are wrapping things up (we are in a way), but you still have another section to read. You still haven't heard how I navigated the unknown and built myself to this point. It may not be Halloween, but I still have plenty of treats to hand out.

# SECTION III: THE MEAT & POTATOES

## SUGAR

Since childhood, I've had a sweet tooth. That probably explains why, to this day, my favorite holiday is Halloween, not because of the costumes, but because of the limitless candy. After quitting alcohol, I indulged in sugar more, especially during binges, leading to feeling sluggish, negative, and unhealthy. I gained weight and developed bad habits like frequent fast-food meals, mainly from McDonald's, and neglecting exercise. Moving helped me cut back, but cravings returned, especially in isolation. Cold turkey works best for me, though emotional challenges trigger sugar cravings. I recently started using a tool to manage binges and realized sugar often fills a need for connection. I'm still working through my sugar dependence, but I'm uncovering important links.

## GAMBLING (WRITTEN IN APRIL 2023)

A week ago today, after my direct deposit paycheck went through, I felt the urge to celebrate the long work week by frequenting the casino in Dodge City, Kansas. I had not been in a few weeks, but the last time I went, I only took out $200 and left the casino $80 up. This time around, I didn't have such luck. Upon arriving at the casino, I took out my $200 allotment, but after a few hours, it was gone entirely. I returned to the ATM a total of four more times, amassing a debt of over $800. I hit one modest jackpot and took home $300, but in the end, I lost $500. It may not seem like much to some, but for me, that was a good chunk of change. I've tried to enforce the firm rule of spending no more than $200 and visiting a casino only when I'm in the company of others, since I am less likely to spiral out of control in the presence of others. As you obviously read, I was unable to stick to either of those rules, and it not only affected my pockets but also my mental health. This recent casino adventure left me in a dejected mood for two days, but also lit a fire under me to get it together. Since becoming sober, I have lost more money to the casino than I had lost in my previous thirty-two years of existence. That may sound like a lot, but you have to remember the fact that I've only been gambling since the age of twenty-one, and some of those years, I could count on one hand how many times I visited a casino.

Spending time journaling my thoughts and difficulties with gambling is the first step in acknowledging I have a problem. It only matters that I believe it is a problem for me. I feel people in general get caught up in validating or invalidating their concerns, issues, or unwanted behaviors based on how they compare to others. I look forward to seeking more information about gambling problems and attacking this issue that has become more prevalent since becoming sober. I have acknowledged it; now I have to put in the work to identify what triggers the behavior that keeps returning to the ATM. I want to gamble as I did in my late twenties, when I would only visit during a celebratory occasion or trip and would stick to my allotted amount. Back then, I knew when to take the loss and call it a night, but lately I have had a hard time sticking to my guns. Gambling has affected my financial freedom and mental health, and if I don't make the necessary changes, it could impact more areas of my life. I cannot and will not let that happen.

## GAMBLING (6 MONTHS LATER)

Knowing a big decision was imminent, my mind started to seek numbing, altering, and pleasure-distracting vices. The urge to drink was alive and well, but I suppressed those thoughts into a dark room. Next in line stood Gambling, with a giant grin on his face. I caved in, and my mind was made up that I was gambling on this humid, windy summer evening. I took out my initial $220 withdrawal once I arrived at the casino and not a penny more. In about an hour, that $220 (birthday money) was gone, and now I stood at the crossroads. I walked up to the ATM, but at the last second I turned around. I walked out of the casino and to my car with a pep in my step. I drove home and later that night made the decision I was alluding to earlier. I was proud of myself for my conduct at the casino, and it reminded me of how I gambled in my younger days. It was a step in the right direction, and it showed me I am capable of gambling responsibly.

## LOVING KINDNESS

While surfing YouTube for meditation videos, I came across a loving-kindness meditation that caught my eye. The old me would have thought this was silly, but this more in-touch-with-my-feelings side had to see what this was all about. After finishing my first loving kindness meditation, I experienced an irresistible urge to text an old girlfriend, and that is precisely what I did. I wasn't seeking a response from her, and I felt secure knowing that. I texted her a script that I had just learned moments before. In the loving-kindness meditation video I watched, I repeated a script directed at three people in my life: one person I care for deeply, one person I see in my everyday life but don't know personally, and one person with whom I've had conflict.

The strongest wave of emotions washed over me when I repeated that script, thinking of that one person with whom I had a conflict. I felt all the pent-up resentment leave my body as I settled into a deep relaxation after reading that script. Dabbling in different meditation practices is something

I've been experimenting with for a few years now. It has brought me calmness and oneness that I haven't been able to replicate. I strongly encourage you, readers, to adopt some form of meditation. All this is to say, I wish you all loving kindness. I had to explain this back story so that I could get to this part.

**MAY YOU BE WELL**
**MAY YOU BE HAPPY**
**MAY YOU BE AT PEACE**
**MAY YOU BE LOVED**

## READING

Growing up, to say I struggled to read is a vast understatement. I started behind and never could catch up to my peers in terms of pace and overall reading skills. Given this developmental delay, I grew a hatred for reading. When we were quizzed on what we read or given book reports in school, I would try my damnedest to skim-read, hoping to get a C. I often hear people bring up books they read in school, whether in middle or high school, and I find myself recalling not a single one. I was in my early twenties when I finished a book from cover to cover. Hopefully I've painted the picture that reading, and I were not two peas in a pod. It might surprise you to learn that I now read for fifteen to twenty minutes, if not more, every day. Reading has become a customary routine in my life. I can't pinpoint the exact moment things changed, but the older I get, the more captured I get. What entices me about reading is the escape you get from everyday life. Reading allows you to see life from another perspective simply by following the words on the page. I don't think my reading skills have changed all that much; I still struggle to sound out particular words at the same leisurely pace.

What has changed is my curiosity about self-growth, and my use of reading as a vehicle for gaining knowledge. I love hearing stories of adversity, struggle, and raw vulnerability in authors. I love seeing the transformation from where people started to where they are now. I love acquiring insight into helpful techniques and lifestyle preferences that have worked for others. The high school me would be shocked to hear me speak so glowingly about reading. I wouldn't say I turned a weakness into a strength, but I would say I changed the way I view reading. Over the years, I have grown to eliminate self-judgment about my abilities and to work on something I struggle with. My advice is to be kind to yourself and always believe in yourself above all. Who knows—something you struggle with now could turn out to be something you love in the future.

From my readings, I want to leave you with a few quotes to ponder. "Everyone doesn't know something, but everyone knows something else. Everyone can't do something, but everyone can do something else" (Langer 232). I love the message behind this quote, and I feel everyone should be subjected to it. Never feel less than anyone because you can't do something; instead, take pride in the things you can do. Neuropsychologist Barbara Sahakian states that "If you're interested in mastery, you have to learn this lesson. To really achieve anything, you have to be able to tolerate and enjoy risk" (Kolter 102). The mastery I'm most interested in is self. I know I'm making progress in the domain of self because of my willingness to take risks. I'm not sure if I'll ever enjoy risk, but maybe one day I'll get there. I have one question for you guys. Are you ready to take some risks? Don't get me wrong, that last question would have made an excellent ending point, but I had to add one last quote. I finished this writing section months ago, but as I was nearing the end of *The Social Animal* by David Brooks, I was taken aback by what I read on the final page. Author David Brooks closes his excellent book by saying, "much of life is about failure, whether we acknowledge it or not, and your destiny is profoundly shaped by how effectively you learn from and adapt to failure" (Brooks 382). Enough said.

# MUSIC

Music holds a special place in my heart because it possibly saved my life. I'll take you back to the summer of 2018 when I was living in Ottawa, Kansas. I had recently graduated from OTA school and had been job-hunting to no avail. I was living in a studio in a building with four units. I paid $550 a month for a rinky-dink apartment that turned out to be cockroach and mice-infested. At the time, I was being financially supported by my Gran and the loans I had taken out. My funds were running low, and week after week was passing without a response to a job opportunity. In the spring of 2018, I broke up with a girlfriend due to the toxic nature of our relationship. The combination of low funds, no job prospects on the horizon, and still recovering from a tumultuous relationship left me at an all-time low.

At that time in my life, I never wanted to show my family I was struggling, and I didn't want to worry them with my trivial issues. As you will soon see, my struggles were a little more than trivial, but that was my mindset at the time. With nowhere to turn for help, I started to develop suicidal thoughts. One night, those thoughts eventually led to taking physical steps: grabbing a butcher knife from my drawer and heading to the bathroom. Before I reached the bathroom, I stopped to grab my iPod to see if I could find any song that represented what I was feeling at the time. A new song that proved profound to the masses left an impression on me. I lay in the bathroom tub, listening to this same song over and over for ten hours, with the butcher knife just outside, within reach. I was able to relate on an emotional level and experience a cathartic release.

Before this experience, I had never gone to music in a low emotional state, and for some reason, I was called to it that day. Music helped me sit with my emotions through support that resonated with my feelings at the time. It made me explore how others would be impacted by my decision and how hurt they would be. I am blessed and grateful to have loved ones in my life who genuinely care about my well-being. I steered away from the suicidal thoughts the more I thought about my loved ones. A few days after this unforgettable day, I got a call back about a job opportunity in southwest Kansas. I jumped at the chance, and within two weeks, I was in southwest Kansas with a new outlook on life. Music is a foundational piece of my everyday existence, and I know I can always turn to music during hard times. At times, I turn to music for inspiration when writing, and hearing about perseverance or struggle empowers me. I didn't always have the motivation to write, and I often found the inspiration I needed through powerful melodies and thought-provoking lyrics. The music set the mood, and my creativity took over. I listened to powerful theme songs like "Cornfield Chase" from the movie Interstellar, alternative rock like Nirvana, and everything in between. For me, it's hard to beat the tranquility you get from going on a walk while listening to music. Music is therapeutic for me, and when you find activities in life that bring you peace, keep them close and don't let go.

If you are experiencing suicidal thoughts, just know there are people out there who will help you. You can always reach out to someone or find a way to express what you're going through. There is a suicide hotline (**1-800-273-8255**), and you can always reach out to me if you need to. You can email me at brengreg1990@yahoo.com, and I can get in touch with you further. You can always turn to someone. YOU MATTER, and YOU ARE LOVED.

## WORK

I can't remember where, but somewhere in this book, I mentioned what I do for a living. If you weren't paying attention or skimmed that part over, I work as a Certified Occupational Therapist Assistant (COTA) at a small rural hospital in southwest Kansas. Most of my work experience in this field has been within a 40-mile radius of southwest Kansas. Since I entered this line of work in 2018, I have found tremendous purpose. For years, my "why" was work and only work. At times in the past, I have distanced myself from family and friends, and the one constant has been work. I really don't know where I would be in life had I not stumbled on this line of work. Having the opportunity to make a difference every day totally aligns with who I am as a person.

Work has given me purpose, structure, social time, and (work) family. It's rare to get all those elements at one job, but working in southwest Kansas has given me everything I could ask for and more. My place of employment has happily taken me in, accepted me, nurtured me, supported me, pushed me, and allowed me to grow. I set out for what I thought were greener pastures a few times, but this pasture gave me everything I needed. When I didn't know who I was or what I wanted to do with my life, work pulled me through tough times and kept my head above water.

In the past year, I've made a conscious effort to have more outside of work. I've realized how important it is to have a good work-life balance, especially when you work in healthcare. Working in healthcare can do a number on your mental health; it's no joke. The longer I've worked in healthcare, the more I've appreciated having paid time off (PTO). Sometimes I need to go on a trip, visit family, or have a personal day to decompress and come back rejuvenated. We spend so much time caring for others that I feel we in healthcare are more prone to mental health issues and burnout. Take care of your well-being, my fellow healthcare professionals.

Another sad byproduct of my occupation is experiencing death. I remember during my first rotation in OTA school, we had a nursing home resident pass away 1 day after I worked with him in therapy. I had a hard time wrapping my head around the idea that I would never see him again. It seemed wild to me that I could work with someone one day and, the next, they would be gone, just like that. Over the years, sadly, I have seen many people come and go. You become desensitized to death, and I honestly don't know if that's a good thing. I understand it's a job, and at the end of the day, I have a job to do, but I feel talking about it is a start. Have any of you in healthcare ever questioned this? I don't want to be so numb to death that I can't properly grieve the loss of someone close to me in the future. It makes me wonder, but I will pore over this topic more intently in the future. Work pushed my creative boundaries.

Working as an Occupational Therapy practitioner means I must constantly think on the fly and create treatment interventions out of thin air (it feels like sometimes). Working a job that continually forces you to evolve your thinking and adapt in the moment has molded my creative talent. Work nurtured my creative abilities, and I wouldn't be writing these words without working in this line of work. All in all, I am truly blessed to do what I do for a living, and I couldn't think of a better place to foster my passion. Sometimes, beggars can't be choosers, and some have to take a job strictly for the income. But if you're so lucky and have the opportunity, find a job that gives you more than you give it. I know I found that job!

## A FORMER PATIENT'S LITTLE SISTER DREW THIS ILLUSTRATION OF ME

# MOMENT #5: MY WORDS ONE WEEK BEFORE ENTERING SOBRIETY

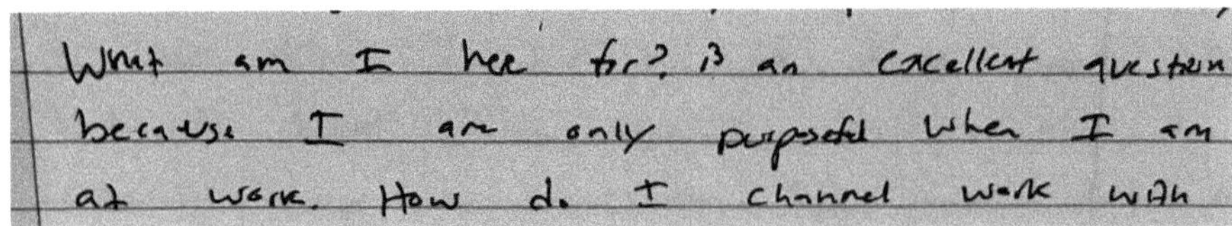

What am I here for? is an excellent question because I am only purposeful when I am at work. How do I channel work with

The fact that I felt I only had purpose when I was working is heartbreaking to reflect on. I feel bad for that version of me, because I am so much more than that. Take it from me, don't put your whole identity into one thing. We are multi-faceted creatures, and a single role or skill doesn't define us. We all possess qualities, characteristics, interests, talents, personality traits, and aspects that make us complex. Each one of us owns a range of abilities and identities.

My mind was so clouded that I couldn't see all the aspects of myself. I honed in on the negatives, and the positives were shrugged off. Work was something I did, but it's certainly not everything I am. Remember, you are so much more than that one thing you do. You may not always see it, but that's why I'm here. I'm here to tell you, you are a versatile individual. It will take deliberate work to view yourself in a more positive light, but I believe you can.

# VOICE MEMOS

Inspiration to write often hits me in the face during the wee hours of the day. The calmness and clarity this time of day lends itself to, sets me up nicely to be at my best. There's one caveat: I continually have to pull the plug on my writing sessions because I have to go to work or, on occasion, have another morning obligation. As I write this, it's the morning of Friday, October 25, 2024, which means I have about fifteen minutes left before I have to get to work. The analogy that comes to my mind when I think about abandoning my writing session is that of bringing a locomotive train (my writing thoughts) to a screeching halt.

Once I get into writing mode, it can be hard to turn off the tsunami of thoughts and ideas that encompass my mind. Back in the spring of 2024, I started recording my thoughts and ideas in voice memos. Luckily, I had a 35-minute drive to work, which gave me plenty of time to round out my thoughts. When I first started, I had a hard time re-listening to the voice memos because I didn't like the way my voice sounded. I critiqued my voice, tone, and speech delivery as if I were speaking to an audience. I've never been the most articulate, and I'd be the first to admit that. Tragically, many equate your intelligence with how well you speak. Surely, you can see this is a topic I feel insecure about. Perhaps my liking of podcasts played a role in how harshly I judged myself. My proclivity to write early in the morning put me in a predicament. I either had to find another time of day to write or embrace recording and re-listening to my voice. I decided to stick to the latter.

Over time, I grew to accept how I sound and how I speak. I started noticing a more reassuring, confident tone, too. That time for voice memos during my 35-minute drive ended in August 2024, when I moved to live in the same town where I worked. I no longer had the hour-long round-trip drive, and my gas budget would benefit. Early mornings are still my peak writing times, and I've improved at finding good stopping points. I like to walk to work (weather permitting), and that gives me roughly fifteen minutes to voice memo if I need to. On occasion, my desire to write lingers on even as I arrive at work. I hope my boss doesn't read this, but a few times I've had to spend my first ten to fifteen minutes at work writing, indiscreetly, I hope.

Trying to make the most of my writing sessions meant I had to get uncomfortable. I forced myself to do something outside my comfort zone to get closer to my goal. Through sheer repetition, I grew to welcome the sound of my voice. Hearing my voice used to make me cringe, but now I know that's just me. I've come a long way in this department, but don't expect me to open on *Saturday Night Live* anytime soon.

## SPEAKING TO THE FELLAS

Ladies, you are more than welcome to follow along, but this writing session is for the fellas. Before I could write with you fellas in mind, I had to overcome some reservations I had when it came to speaking freely to another man. Some of you fellas might agree, but it is so much easier to have a heart-to-heart talk with a woman. I feel more comfortable conversing with women than with men. I have been very reluctant to share my feelings with men for a myriad of reasons. I'm having a hard time writing this right now, if I'm being candid. I can't help but resort to my old way of thinking when it comes to this topic. I feel like I'm being judged by all the fellas out there as weak, sensitive, and soft right now. I also know I have a strong message to deliver, and I must move past my insecurities. I'm willing to take the bullet of being labeled negatively if it hits home for someone else out there. I want you fellas to know I don't judge you for how you feel, and if you ever need someone to talk to, I'm always free to listen. Talking freely to another man wasn't a part of our past, but it doesn't have to be our future.

A lot of men are struggling out there, and we need to find a way to have meaningful conversations. Behind that macho bravado is a man seeking a deep emotional connection with another man. Whether that's buddies that grew up together, college roommates (like Aric and me), or coworkers, we could use support from another man. When I say we, I'm also referring to myself. I've been able to have some open talks with men recently, but getting me to do that is like pulling teeth. It does not come naturally, but I'm willing to work on it.

Writing on this topic is a start. Let's support our fellas on an emotional level. Forget everything we learned from our past, and let's be there for each other. To all you fellas out there, I care about your feelings, and I want you to be more receptive towards other fellas. Let's take it a step further. Not long after you read this, I want you to send a text, call, or meet face-to-face with another man and express some of the things I mentioned above. Ask them how they're really doing. If you can't do that, let them know you are always available to talk if they ever need to. Let them know you were thinking of them, and you just wanted to check in. However you go about it, make sure they feel cared about by another man. I know it can feel uncomfortable, but put your ego aside and be there for a fellow man. You could really make someone's day, remember that.

## INSPIRATION MAGNIFIED

An abundance of inspiration can be observed in our daily lives. Although those inspirational reels on social media can be of value, let's stop scrolling for a second. Over the last year, I have written letters to people who have inspired me. These people are public figures who have made significant contributions to their fields. Think of highly distinguished writers and generational music talents that have moved the needle in society. Innately, this is not uncommon, but for me, it was a moment of discovery. In the past, my insecurities kept me from praising anyone. Instead, I've been more likely to rain on someone's parade, inwardly, of course.

I was envious of specific figures who could be themselves or who carved out their own lane. Behind closed doors, I admired who they were, but my pride held me back from accepting their contributions. During this discovery process, it became abundantly clear that I would ignore anything inspirational. I didn't feel worthy of inspiration, and I never thought it would amount to much anyway. Boy, was I wrong.

I'm in the midst of an inspirational renaissance in my life. I find inspiration in documentaries, books, stories of adversity, music, people, behaviors, and small gestures. I want to start normalizing praise for the common man or woman who overcame a challenging obstacle. I draw a lot of inspiration from my family and others in my life. For example, I have a friend who recently embarked on a new endeavor, and I texted her some helpful practices to keep in mind as she makes a change. A few weeks later, she sent me a text saying she had worked out for the last three days, which helped her relieve some stress. She ended the text with "Thank you for the advice." I was in a lull that week, and her text inspired me to go to the gym that same night. Five days later, I sent her this text.

I had an off week myself and I just wanted to say your message during the week gave me some inspiration to get a workout in that night! Thanks for inspiring me.

I don't hesitate to let people know when they have inspired me. I take the inspiration I gain from others and use it to inspire you. Don't just settle for inspiration alone; it has to be followed by action. Inspiration gets you to the starting line of change, but the action of running the race leads to change.

When I think about it, inspiration can be found anytime and anywhere. The analogy that's buzzing around in my head revolves around bees. A bee feeds on nectar and pollen (inspiration), which are vital nutrients for its development. We sometimes need to feed on inspiration to drive action that can lead to personal growth. Bees inadvertently carry pollen (inspiration) from one flower (human) to another, which in turn promotes genetic diversity and more adaptable offspring. We need to take those remnants of inspiration we've acquired and give back to the people around us. This can be done unintentionally simply by being yourself. We all have the capacity to inspire people by breathing life into someone who was once lifeless.

We can use our voices and insights to expand someone's horizons or lift someone up. Before this can happen, you have to make yourself available to being inspired. Stay humble, unassuming, and open. Don't disregard the little things. It could be a word you said, a look you gave, a text you sent, or a phone call you made that could inspire someone. "When you need encouragement, think of the qualities the people around you have: this one's energy, that one's modesty, another's generosity, and so on. Nothing is as encouraging as when virtues are visibly embodied in the people around us, when we're practically showered with them. It's good to keep this in mind" (Aurelius, Meditations 6.48)

## KEEP A FEW RECEIPTS

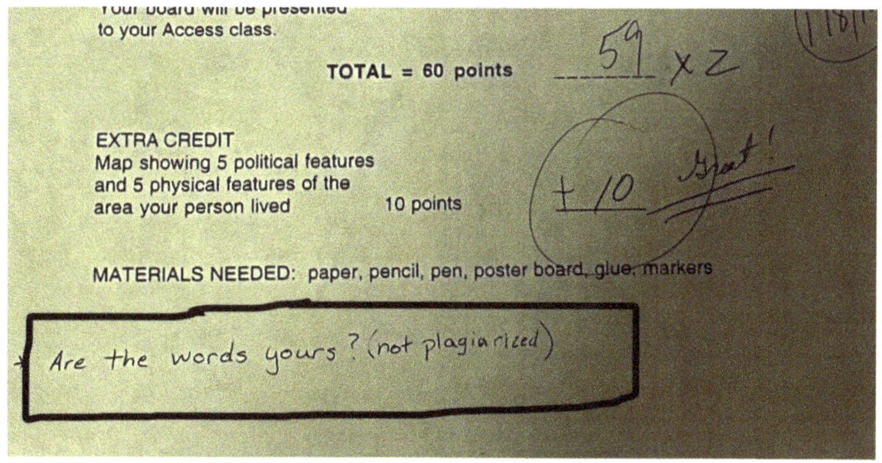

to your Access class.

TOTAL = 60 points 59 x 2

EXTRA CREDIT
Map showing 5 political features and 5 physical features of the area your person lived 10 points +10 Great!

MATERIALS NEEDED: paper, pencil, pen, poster board, glue, markers

Are the words yours? (not plagiarized)

The grading rubric above is from a project I worked on in 6th grade. As you can see, I was 1 point away from having a perfect score. While the teacher gave me a very satisfactory grade, it's clear to see my abilities were being called into question. I recently found this grading rubric while going through some old storage boxes, and man, did it stick out like a sore thumb. I don't have any ill will towards the teacher (who I can't remember anyway), but I needed to see this. I need reminders why I'm going to write this book, and it adds some kerosene to my already well-lit fire. While I believe your drive for growth should come from within, I also think that at certain times, growth can be driven by outside influences. I believe it's important to walk a fine line when it comes to outside influences, but there's still room for them. I wouldn't let others' opinions consume you, but when you feel questioned or doubted, review those receipts. Self-ignite your fire, but use external motivators to keep the embers burning when you don't have it internally.

## YOU'RE MORE RESILIENT THAN YOU THINK

Last night, I was reading a journal entry from late March 2020 (the start of COVID-19), in which I reflected on a stormy relationship. I'll spare you from reading the entire 3-page entry, but I have included a snippet that brings home my point. I'll talk first, and then you can read the little snippet. It's safe to say that all of us have had a moment or two in life where we had to face uncertainty eye to eye, and we somehow came out on the other side. We unwittingly trudge forward, because that's all we know. Pure resolve and adaptability are what make us unique. For Pete's sake, look how far we (humans) have come since the beginning of time.

We are stronger and more resilient than we think. We should keep visual reminders or mementos of resiliency to help recall. I'm not saying you should revisit traumatic events in your life, but you should revisit how you felt when you overcame that trying situation. Keep these relics of resiliency in a safe and easily accessible place. Remember how you've arrived at this point in life. Whether it's a battle scar or a small callus, take pride in your ability to overcome what you never imagined you could.

# RELICS OF RESILIENCE

At times when I thought I could never move on or I couldn't live here without her, I did! I have surprised myself and I am so much healthier both mentally and physically because I didn't let this situation get the best of me. I showed true grit and determination to turn my life aroud for my betterment. I want to encourage people to grow and show resilence during difficult times. Things will get bette

# FIVE TRAVEL ESSENTIALS ON MY SELF-DISCOVERY JOURNEY

## EXPRESS YOURSELF

I've questioned the validity at times, but I've shown a natural aptitude for writing. Not any old writing, but writing as a means of expression. Back in the day, when I entered an emotional state, I would turn to the bottle to cope. Nowadays, I turn to pen and paper or laptop and keyboard during emotional states. My identity has transformed from a volatile drinker to a serene writer in a matter of a few years. Expressing myself vocally has not always been a strength of mine, and I've accepted that. We all love those people who can express their thoughts, feelings, opinions, and perspectives with confidence, but not everyone operates that way.

Over time, I've embraced my preferred way of expressing myself while also finding my voice. I have made tremendous strides in sharing vocally with others, and I'm light-years ahead of where I was. Nothing gives me superpowers quite like writing does. Writing has unlocked a level of passion in me I didn't know I possessed. Since that day in April 2024, I have obsessively pursued the writing of this book. I've never felt so driven and determined in my life. Writing has given me a new sense of self. Once you get wise to who you are, you start to look at yourself differently. You carry yourself with more confidence, and that confidence oozes into everything you do. Writing is my baby, and I'm not just a writer. I'm a storyteller, a creator, and a visionary. I'm all of these things, so don't limit yourself to one form of self-expression.

What's your preferred form of expressing yourself? Not everyone can express themselves vocally, and that's okay. Have you truly contemplated what form of expression calls out to you? You may not know, and that's also okay. You might be one life-altering decision away from discovering yourself. In the meantime, I want you to explore and trial all the forms of expression you have at your disposal. Some quick forms of expression that come to mind include journaling (first and foremost), poetry, art, dance, fashion, music, etc. Please find that form of expression that rings true to you. Finally, how can your form of self-expression impact others?

## WORD OF ADVICE: GIVE BACK

I may not be a motivational speaker, but I am The Awakened Creator. I use my strongest form of self-expression as a productive outlet and to inspire others. Find your niche in self-expression and find a way to help others. It may be a simple word, a note of encouragement, or something on a grand scale, like writing a book. Whether it has a high-profile impact on the masses or not, I want you to share your perspective and insights with the intention of helping. No matter how insignificant you may feel at times, someone out there could benefit from your viewpoint, your advice, or your presence.

## KEEP A SECRET

As I write this, nobody knows I'm writing this book. Years ago, when I first caught the writing bug, I told some people about my aspirations to write a book. My statements were met with skepticism, and I retreated. Writing a book at that time never picked up steam, and I quickly jumped ship. I frequently share with others that I journal, but nobody knows I'm creating a work of art as we speak. I've committed to working in silence.

The hardest decision I've made has been to keep this book a secret. You have no idea how bad I want to express my passion for this project with those close to me. Keeping this book a secret has pushed me to extremes. I've devised a few contingency plans to ensure I won't take my book to the grave with me. It's important to err on the side of caution with priceless material. Keeping my work in its purest form, free from outside noise, is a must. I don't want the essence of this book affected by positive or negative comments. So, I've decided to turn inward.

Inward I turned, but as time wore on, I experienced a rise in self-belief that shifted my perspective on secrecy. I eventually told a handful of people my intentions for writing this book. I couldn't contain all the excitement to myself, and I've reached the level where outside noises don't affect me as much. I still move in silence, but this time around, you might hear some creaks and cracks.

## WORD OF ADVICE: GROW IN SILENCE

There is nothing wrong with letting people know about your efforts at self-improvement, but, more than anything, grow in silence. Growing internally far outweighs any external growth you receive; remember that. Sometimes we need to shut our mouths and get to work. Keeping your work within keeps it sacred and free from ridicule. In his song "*Too Deep for the Intro,*" J. Cole goes on to say, "If they don't know your dreams, then they can't shoot 'em down." Celebrating the fruits of your labor with those close to you will only feel that much sweeter after the fact. If you strengthen your self-belief muscle to the point where nothing can derail your destiny, then feel free to share with others. Even then, I would be thoughtful about who you decide to share your vision with. Surround yourself with others who lift you and bring positivity to your life. On the flip side, never let anyone set your limits or decide your potential. You are limitless, and you manage your potential. The only person standing in the way of accomplishing your goals is you. If you decide to share with others and things go awry, you can always withdraw to your lair in obscurity.

# MOMENT #6: CONTINGENCY PLAN

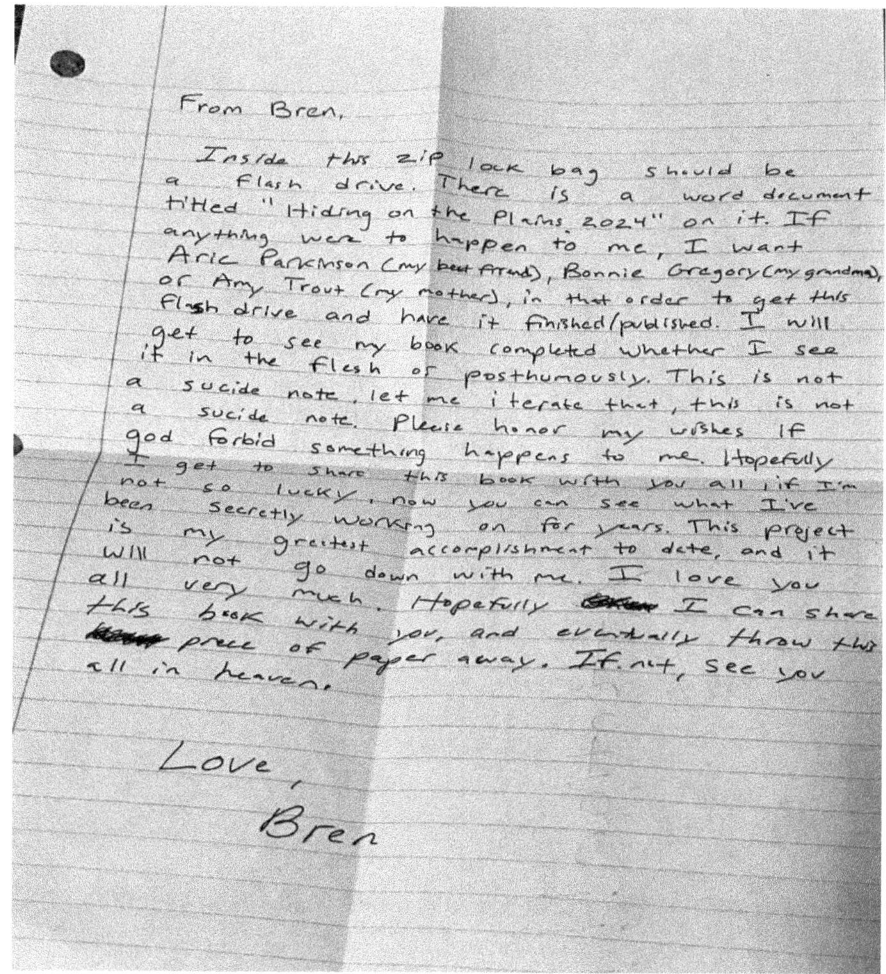

From Bren,

Inside this zip lock bag should be a flash drive. There is a word document titled "Hiding on the Plains 2024" on it. If anything were to happen to me, I want Aric Parkinson (my best friend), Bonnie Gregory (my grandma), or Amy Trout (my mother), in that order to get this flash drive and have it finished/published. I will get to see my book completed whether I see it in the flesh or posthumously. This is not a sucide note, let me iterate that, this is not a sucide note. Please honor my wishes if god forbid something happens to me. Hopefully I get to share this book with you all, if I'm not so lucky, now you can see what I've been secretly working on for years. This project is my greatest accomplishment to date, and it will not go down with me. I love you all very much. Hopefully I can share this book with you, and eventually throw this piece of paper away. If not, see you all in heaven.

Love,

Bren

This letter was included to show you my commitment to my vision. Sharing my story for my sake and for others was undeniable. This serves as a reminder that you might have to go to great lengths to fulfill your dreams. Plan and watch for pitfalls!

## FIND TIME FOR REFLECTION

Even before sobriety, I set aside some time every Sunday for a reflection routine. Initially, the routine consisted of writing goals, gratitude, and reflecting on the week. It was a routine I pieced together through books I read, and it seemed like a grounding activity. At first, I was going through the motions, just to mark it off my to-do list. Over time, I found my rhythm for writing in a reflective state, and it soon became a weekly must. Writing weekly goals or priorities didn't seem to help me much, so I scratched that idea. You can only be grateful for your family, job, and home so many times before you start to question "What am I doing?" My gratitude practice began to expand as I reflected on grateful interactions and feelings of gratitude I experienced during the week. Even in the worst situations, you can always find a glimmer of gratitude. My weekly reflection, as I like to call it, has transformed considerably since I started, and I can't imagine not doing it once a week. I used to write a summary of what I did during the week, and I was clearly missing the point. Through practice, I started writing about my key takeaways, highs and lows, and areas for improvement. It was a time when I could be brutally honest about my shortcomings while also acknowledging areas for growth. It was the one time every week I could write without judging myself too harshly. Having a reflection routine has been a form of therapy for me.

## WORD OF ADVICE: DEVELOP A REFLECTION ROUTINE

If you don't already have a reflection routine, be open and curious to developing one. You may have to experiment to learn which techniques and forms work best for you. My reflective writing practice may not work for you, and that's fine. Maybe a self-talk reflection in your head or out loud while recording a voice memo works for you. It may be a weekly call to a specific person that gives you that reflective time. You artsy folks might get reflection in other activities, and that's a beautiful thing. Find the method that works best for you and stick with it. Check in with yourself about where you are and where you're trying to go. Make this check-in a staple in your reflection routine. Whether it's once a day, once a week, or once a month, develop and cultivate a reflection routine that suits you. Find a time when you can be honest with yourself without being overly judgmental. Having a reflection routine will be essential for those of you going through a transformative time in your life.

## WELCOME FEAR

"Stop being afraid of being afraid" is a quote I heard recently that had me questioning my own fears. What do I fear? I think the question should be the other way around: what don't I fear? I fear being alone and having no companionship. I fear rejection. This fear has withstood the test of time. I can remember so many incidents in my life where I was scared to do something for fear of rejection. Rejection from my family, friends, work acquaintances, and rejection from a girl. In my case, a girl, but whether it's a girl or a boy, we have all experienced rejection in some form or fashion.

It's funny to me that I say I don't care what people think of me, and yet my fears strongly disagree. Fear of conflict is another fear I have that has been with me my whole life. I don't like to ruffle anyone's feathers, and I'll often go out of my way to avoid conflict. So, I keep my mouth shut and absorb the blow of not expressing my true feelings. These blows can take a toll, building up tension when I get upset with myself for not speaking my mind. I will say the topic of conflict has improved, but it is still a fear of mine and something I still struggle with.

Through writing, I've been able to pinpoint many of my fears. Accepting my fears and growing as a person has empowered me to face them head-on. The fact that you are reading this book shows that I overcame a fear. Before we leave, I want to share all my worries with you. I FEAR dying alone, not fulfilling my potential, distancing myself from my loved ones, disappointing or bringing embarrassment to the ones I love, things going wrong in my life, resorting to my old ways, being a fraud, letting people down, conformity, conflict, rejection, and alcohol disorder.

## WORD OF ADVICE: GRAB "FEAR" BY THE HORNS

Fear is inevitable and afflicts us all. Some of us have more fears than others, but they nonetheless influence us all. I want you to mindfully consider your fears and find a way to monitor them over time. Fears don't necessarily have to be a bad thing; we can use them to learn a lot about ourselves. You can either be frozen by fear or driven by fear; what you decide is up to you. George Addair said it beautifully when he said, "Everything you ever wanted is on the other side of fear."

## BELONG TO YOURSELF

While on a walk listening to music, the question of "where do I belong?" dawned on me. To a certain degree, I always felt like the oddball—the outcast —different from my family, friends, and peers. For years, I pondered if I was adopted, even given the strong resemblance I share with my dad. I didn't have the words to voice these thoughts, but they persisted for years. I hated not fitting in, and I constantly questioned myself. What about me made it so challenging to immerse myself with those close to me? Why did God create me with such poor interpersonal skills, along with my already inadequate intrapersonal skills? For years, I shunned myself for the way I was and yearned for understanding. I viewed myself negatively compared to those close to me. Sobriety led to a seismic shift in how I approach belonging. I have embraced the variety of traits I possess as a human being.

I now understand what I bring to this world: kindness, compassion, and empathy. My lax attitude and open-mindedness don't fit everyone's ideology, and I've come to grips with that. My uniqueness and creativity enabled me to share my story. It's one thing to accept who you are, but it's another thing to feel comfortable where you stand. I finally feel comfortable in my own shoes with little room to spare. I found a way to believe in myself, whether other people did or not. Nobody knows I'm writing this book, but if they did, there's no question I would have some doubters. In all actuality, until recently, I never believed in myself, so how can I expect others to believe in me? The person I want to be and the person I am both belong to me. Once I addressed where I stood with myself, I could then turn my sights to others. Instead of overthinking our differences, I've highlighted the similarities I share with those I love. Over the years, my social group has declined in numbers, but with that has come a stronger connection and commitment to those in my life.

## WORD OF ADVICE: YOU BELONG.

Above all, I want you to know you aren't alone when it comes to feelings of belonging. Remember, we're all fighting silent battles, even those who seem perfect on the surface. At the end of the day, you belong, and I want you to take pride in that. Believing in yourself starts within, and you must rely on yourself to fuel that belief. Belonging is a feeling, and you will know right away whether you belong. Don't change who you are to fit in, but rather seek people who fit you. Remember, when it comes to relationships, focus on quality over quantity. Even at your loneliest, I want you to remember that you matter and you belong. Whether it's from far or close, I want you to know that I will sit with you. We all have our own pains and struggles. I'm not looking to change you, fix you, lecture to you, or shame you right now. There's a time and place for that, but a lot of us just need someone to sit with us in our pain. Remember, we all have a place in this world, and if I found my place, I know you can too.

# THE GRAND CRESCENDO

We're rounding third base and heading home, but before we do, I have some last-minute advice to spew. Most of my advice was learned through life experiences or concepts I came to understand over time. I diverge from my own advice daily, and it takes steadfast resolve to challenge your old way of thinking. Things won't always go the way you want, but you must commit to a growth mindset. Challenge is a prerequisite if you want to grow, and if you're aware of that, you'll be on your way. On your way to tapping into your inherent, unbounded potential.

Let's avoid comparing our life circumstances to others'. It can help you gain perspective, but it doesn't lead to change. We tend to gauge our worth in life by how we stack up against others. I told myself for years that my issues were minuscule compared to others, and while I agree, that didn't help me address my issues. That comparative mindset I carried served as a cop-out for many years. I feel blessed for the life I have lived so far, but I also need to address some areas in my life. Some people didn't think my drinking issues were that bad (maybe they didn't see my bad nights, or they had seen worse), but to me, it was a glaring concern.

Not everyone will understand your journey of self-improvement, and that's okay. You don't need to explain yourself to anyone, and some people may not like that you are changing right before their eyes. I think that says more about them than it does about you. In my situation, I felt things were dire, and that's all that matters. It was so glaring that getting sober felt like a do-or-die decision to me. I truly felt my life could go off the rails, and I would end up in jail or dead in a ditch somewhere. That fear fueled my determination for change. Even with that said, it takes time for you to realize things aren't working. You must enter that threshold where you're willing to enter the dark to leave your old life. True courage to me is being afraid and charging into the darkness anyway. Identify and address those areas you feel need your attention, regardless of what others think. Nobody knows what it feels like to walk a day in your shoes, and you decide what changes you need to make. Change truly boils down to wanting to and understanding. Gain a clear picture of what changes you want to make in your life.

Acknowledge your growth, no matter how small it may seem. Learn to celebrate and acknowledge your successes. What you overcome may not seem like much to others, but to you it could be a miracle. Let's do away with comparing who overcame more, who had it worse, and this and that. Instead, let's congratulate growth in others, too, no matter how small or large. As a matter of fact, I'm going to do that right now. To anyone reading this book who has overcome something challenging, I want to congratulate you. I am proud of you, and I'm sure you learned a lot about yourself. I believe we are always stronger and more capable than we think.

I forget how that quote goes, but it goes something like, "There is no perfect time to start, but rather starting is the perfect time." I apologize if I butchered that quote, but you get the gist of what I'm trying to say. Don't let things get to the absolute worst before you decide to make a change. Sometimes experiencing the lowest of lows is needed to galvanize change, but it doesn't always have to be. If you feel things are going sideways in life, then start the process of correcting that. It will be uncomfortable, but stay committed to the idea of change. It won't be a smooth sail, but continue to adapt and learn. If it happens, it happens, but you don't have to wait for a do-or-die moment to make a change.

Attain the unattainable. Writing this book once seemed unattainable. For years, I never possessed the self-belief to give it a legitimate go. I was so immersed in how I thought others would perceive me and my book. The herculean effort required to write a book was something I thought I wasn't built to do. It turns out I was built to do the once-unattainable. To believe, you have to start, but don't stop there. To grow that inner belief, you must accelerate and push through the challenges. To sustain that belief, finish what you started. Visualize, visualize, visualize: it can't hurt. Keep that belief fire lit day and night. Belief is built, not given. You are built to attain the once unattainable. Have daily visual, auditory, or tactile reminders of what you are building towards. I looked at my book cover nearly every day to remind myself what I was going to do. Never lose hope in what you're working towards.

We are either consuming or producing information, especially in this digital age. We all routinely consume information, but what are you creating for others? There is great benefit in consuming useful information that can impact your life, like my book, for example, which I hope is having an impact on you. We're all guilty, including myself, of consuming too many hours of content or information that doesn't benefit us. Nothing wrong with it, but could we cut back on consumption and find a way to produce more? It doesn't mean you have to create content in the typical sense on social media, or have a platform (like a podcast, radio show, book, or speaking gig), even though those are great ways to share your perspective. It could be writing a handwritten letter to someone you care about; volunteering your time/expertise to others; or sharing a form of self-expression, like writing, art, comedy, or music, to benefit others.

Whatever you create, we need your voice, your thoughts, your perspective, and your creativity in this world. Follow your heart, make what you feel is right at the time, and adjust as needed. Don't overthink it; do what feels most natural and what feels genuine to you. Creating from a place of authenticity will draw the "right people" to connect with your work. Don't create from a place of animosity where your emotions are invested in the outcome. If I have anyone out there who's aspired to do something, now is the perfect time to start. I believe in your abilities, and you'll be amazed by what you learn about yourself once you go through the process. Everything you need is already in you, but it's up to you to tap into that potential. You must be open to learning, adapting, and creating. The buck stops with you, because you control what you make of your life. Find what's authentically you, and share it with the world.

No being on this planet is perfect, so striving for perfection isn't realistic. "Perfect" indicates zero flaws, but nothing in life is perfect. Now, just because you accept that doesn't mean you have to settle for those imperfections. Strive for improvement and progress. While the majority seek effortless perfection, I strive to be imperfectly hard-working. I think that's a more helpful approach. What do you think? Let's get back to working for the things we want in life. It feels so much better when you put in the work. On a similar note, let's talk about the word success.

I know social media shoves success into our faces ad nauseam, but who determines what success is? To me, success is measured in the eyes of the beholder. You might feel you're lacking in the department of success when you line yourself up with others, but what about those who have less than you; have you thought of them? There are people out there who would die to be in your shoes, so I guess now is a good time to keep a good perspective. Back to our regularly scheduled programming: who controls the narrative around success? You do; success is a feeling, and last time I checked, there was no measurable way to define success. Even if there is, who cares, because at the end of the day, it's a seven-letter word that you attach meaning to. If you need to fuel the fire by telling yourself you aren't successful, don't let me stop you, but it's not necessary. I would caution you to avoid putting too much stock in a word and instead live a life that makes you proud. I'll take a life I'm proud of over a successful life any day of the week, but that's just me (I wish I could insert the shrug emoji).

I'm guilty as charged of waiting for the "right day" for most of my life. For years, I put off doing something because I was looking for the ideal time. There is no perfect time to start or wait for something to happen. Go, start, do, and adjust on the fly. Please don't count the days; make the most of your days, they aren't guaranteed. I know it's cliché, but we ought to be grateful for every day we have. Every day is an opportunity to improve (mentally, physically, emotionally, spiritually), a chance to love, an opportunity to reflect, a willingness to learn, and endless more opportunities.

Dig your heels in when you're ready to commit. When I stepped back from this book, I discovered an underground theme that's now been brought to the surface. This book served as a dartboard for me. The phrase "don't knock until you try it" remained in my psyche while I sought understanding. I'm throwing darts at the board and doubling down on the darts that stick. Some things contributed to my growth, and others were deemed ineffective. After I found those darts that stuck, I went up to the board with a hammer in hand, ready to drive those darts further in. This book served as a forum for me to reinforce my transitional beliefs and values. I found security in sharpening my tools, in shaping my creativity, and holding my ground. The constant reframing and re-expressing was my way of strengthening my core belief. When you find a self-belief that sticks, double, triple, heck, quadruple down on it. Shower yourself with conviction and reinforcement to lay claim to that strong belief.

Find something to hold on to. When I felt I didn't have much I could rely on, not drinking became a badge of honor for me. It gave me hope in those early days of sobriety that I could eventually get to a better place. When everything seemed temporary and fluid, having that one anchor gave me some stability. Be proud of the changes you've made in your life, and delight in facing uncertainty. It's worth noting (no, literally, make a note of this): to grow, you're going to have to take some risks.

I'll be your voice right now, but I'm going to need something from you in the future. If you can't, don't want to, or aren't ready to share your voice, I can be your voice. A goal of mine is to one day have you expand on your own hardships when the time is right. I can handle the workload that comes with being the voice of others because I was destined to do this work. While I speak for you now, I need you to speak for someone else later. I'll let you decide how you approach that moment, but I need you to speak for someone else. When you arrive at that point (because you will), give a piece of you to help others. So many of us can be helped or guided by everyday people (nothing against experts, celebs, or entertainers).

Find practices that jibe with you. I share the practices that helped me, but that's just to give you some early options. Continue seeking practices that bring you what you're ultimately looking for: growth. Keep an open mind, be curious, experiment, explore, and take some shots in the dark. Minimize those preconceived notions and biases, and try, try, try. Throw the dice; can it be any worse than where your life is right now or has been in the past? Life's a crapshoot; you never know what you might find in terms of purpose or hidden passions. Nobody likes to be backed into a corner, and yet so many of us back ourselves into a corner. A corner that limits our choices and traps us like a caged animal. Now is the time to break free of that self-imposed straitjacket we continue to wear day after day. If not today, then when? There could be a treasure trove of resources out there specifically for you, but you must develop a powerful urge for growth.

Be willing to go down some unmarked roads. During your self-discovery journey, you might experience a time when you feel you are being pulled in different directions, but that isn't necessarily a bad thing. I know for me personally, when I started pursuing my creative endeavors, new projects began popping up as my mind went from one idea to the next. I had long breaks from writing this book as I poured more time into other projects that captivated me. I never lost sight of my main project, but I devoted my energy to where my thoughts went at the time. Don't limit the number of avenues you could explore and follow what demands your attention. A lot of my side projects were ideas that emerged from the hidden depths of this book. You may gain a greater or equal purpose going down that road you never envisioned yourself going down. We all have unique journeys that lead us down unscheduled and unexpected roads. In his book *Hidden Potential: The Science of Achieving Greater Things,* author Adam Grant drives home this point beautifully when he says, "we need to embrace the discomfort of getting lost" (Grant 110).

Minimize distractions, and give yourself more of your time. Take the time to invest in yourself. Continue to pursue the best version of you. Clear the static from your radio. Free your mind of distractions and outside noises. Find that frequency that gives you the most clarity. Seek that clear connection. The answers you seek will come if you're tuned into the right frequency.

Don't get hung up on activities that don't nurture you in any way, just because they work for the populace. At times, I fell into the trap of thinking I should be doing x, y, and z. I felt pressured to take the normal (whatever that means) course of action, and I had to mentally capitulate to regain control of the wheel. My calling centers around creation, with this book serving as my greatest virtuoso. This is my *Mona Lisa* masterpiece, my Queen performing at Live Aid moment, and my *In Cold Blood* by Truman Capote classic. Carry self-assuredness when it comes to doing things you like and that work for you. Adopt an empirical mindset when exploring yourself.

Learn through experience. I can't stress this enough: don't be afraid to experiment. Refine your strengths and remedy your weaknesses. Spend more time highlighting the things you are and less time entertaining the things you aren't. Everything's not meant to be a part of your story. In the same vein, everyone's not meant to be in your life. Don't ever write off what you bring to this world because of something you aren't. Always start within and work your way outward, never the other way around. Pursue those lost-in-time passions where you enter a flow-like trance. Those passions that reach out and yank you by the collar ought to be met with open arms. My love for writing grew, and my essence yearned to write. Sometimes I would go a week without writing, and that usually led to dreams about writing concepts. If I weren't always consciously called to write, my subconscious would set me straight and remind me of my calling. When you take hold of your passions in life, cling on.

That's all, folks! Before I close this book out, I want to thank you for following me on my journey. This book was my way of leaving a mark on this world, and I hope you were able to glean something from it. I could end this book in a million ways, but I think I found the perfect send-off. I opted for a quote that was literally music to my ears. To quote lyrics from the song "So Fresh, So Clean" by OutKast, "I love who you are, love who you ain't." Peace!

# ACKNOWLEDGEMENTS, AKA THE WONDERS OF MY WORLD

Thank you, Mom. What you represent as a person—fortitude—is something I strive to achieve myself. When I think of you, I think of work ethic, determination, and drive. You have worked extremely hard to be the very best person you can be for your kids and grandkids. I still remember those days when you felt overwhelmed and tried to get a few moments to yourself, which reminds me of your maternal drive. You always found a way to give us everything we needed. You didn't make excuses or blame others; you simply found a way. You were my first love, and you will always be my strongest love. I love you, Mom, and I hope I make you proud.

Thank you, Gran. Over the years, you told me on several occasions that I was a good writer. When my GPA or grades reflected my incompetence in school, you were the only person who told me I was great at writing. So much of the feedback I received highlighted my deficits, but early on, you saw that I had some writing talent. You believed in me and gave me confidence when I had little in the tank. It wasn't hard to spot my lack of confidence in those years, and you gave me something to hang my hat on. Thank you for the example you set, Gran. In my 34 years, no one has had a greater impact on me than you. I learned many of my daily and weekly routines simply by watching how you operate. Thank you for your mentorship when I was in school all those years ago. I saw how much you enjoyed proofreading and editing my schoolwork. You challenged me to become a better writer. I know one of your goals was to write a book, and you may not be able to accomplish it, but you can experience it through me. I want you to know your mentorship played a big role in making this book possible. Thank you for your love, your wisdom, and the quiet ways you made life better. I hope you know how much you mean to me. I love you, Gran, YOU ARE MY HERO!

Thank you, Dad. Thank you for being a consistent fixture in my life and someone I can always depend on. I want to apologize to you, Dad, for expecting you to be someone else. I compared you and Mom a lot, and I didn't grasp that you expressed your love for me in different ways. Because you didn't love me like Mom, I often overlooked the care and love you gave me. I was too immature to realize that love is not always in the words you say or the physical gestures you make, but rather in the actions you take. You taught me right from wrong, you taught me how to cook a meal, you listened to me talk about my day after school, you showed me how to shoot a basketball, you were my biggest role model, and you prepared me for the real world. I looked up to you so much (still do), and seeking your approval means a lot to me. I'm sorry I didn't appreciate all the love you gave me at times, and now I see all the sacrifices you made for my brothers and me. I love you, Dad.

Thank you, siblings. I've strived to be the best big brother I could, and at times I have fallen woefully short. I'm sorry I've been distant at times, or I haven't checked in as frequently as I should. I am proud of the human beings all four of you have become, and of the roles you play in our family. Thank you for the love you've shown me all our lives, and I hope I have made you all proud. All four of you have many talents and gifts, and I want you guys to pursue those things you are passionate about. I'm always here for you guys and more than willing to help. I think sometime in the distant future I will plan a trip where all four of us can go somewhere, and that sounds cool. I love you all very much.

Thank you to my other immediate family members. Thank you to my Aunt B. The way you progressed in your career has always been something I've admired about you. The impact you've had on so many is something I strive to do myself. Thank you for all the support, guidance, and love over the years. I love you, Aunt B. Thank you to my cousin Ken. You are another brother to me, Ken, and you were my partner in crime (literally that one time). I know we don't see each other much, but I'm proud of the man you've become. The way you give back to the younger generation through teaching is inspiring. You are a smart and talented individual who could have pursued a more lucrative career, but instead chose to give back to the community you grew up in. I love you, Ken. Thank you to all my other family members. I love you all.

Thank you, Aric. Thank you for being a loyal and consistent friend since the day we met. I appreciate you fighting for our friendship early on and always having my back. I appreciate you standing up for me and protecting me from myself during some of my bad nights. When I felt like isolating from everyone, you were the one person who always reached out and broke through my isolating ways. I never knew you could be so close to someone who isn't blood. I'm appreciative of the friendship and brotherhood we have. You are as genuine as they come and bring joy to so many. I'm always here for you, and I love you.

Thank you to all my friends, co-workers, acquaintances, and people who contributed to my development and helped me along the way—those who brought positivity and insight into my life. I appreciate every single person I've encountered in my life, because it takes a group of people for something like this to materialize.

# WORKS CITED


Aurelius, Marcus. *Meditations*. New York: Modern Library, 2002.

Brooks, David. *The Social Animal*. London: Short Books, 2012.

Cole, J. "Too Deep for the Intro." Track on *Friday Night Lights*. Dreamville, Roc Nation, and Columbia, 2010.

Grant, Adam. *Hidden Potential*. New York: Penguin, 2023.

Heider, John. *The Tao of Leadership: Lao Tzu's Tao Te Ching Adapted for a New Age*. Santa Fe, NM: Green Dragon Books, 2015.

OutKast. "So Fresh, So Clean." Track on *Stankonia*. LaFace and Arista, 2000.

Reynard, Sylvain. *Gabriel's Rapture*. New York: Penguin, 2012.

Kotler, Steven. *The Rise of Superman: Decoding the Science of Ultimate Human Performance*. Boston and New York: New Harvest, 2014.

Langer, Ellen J. *The Mindful Body*. New York: Ballantine Books, 2023.

# About the Author

Brennen Gregory is an independent author, who refers to himself as The Awakened Creator. He enjoys watching sports, reading, and working on creative projects. Brennen works as a Certified Occupational Therapy Assistant and lives in St. Joseph, MO.

**You can connect with me on:**

- https://www.instagram.com/bgregory1990
- https://www.facebook.com/brennen.gregory
- https://www.theawakenedcreatorbg.com

www.ingramcontent.com/pod-product-compliance
Lightning Source LLC
LaVergne TN
LVHW021128160826
845679LV00015B/1685